THE EMPLOYMENT SITUATION — NOVEMBER 2013

The **unemployment rate** declined from 7.3 percent to 7.0 percent in November, and total **nonfarm payroll employment** rose by 203,000, the U.S. Bureau of Labor Statistics reported today. Employment increased in transportation and warehousing, health care, and manufacturing.

Chart 1. Unemployment rate, seasonally adjusted, November 2011 – November 2013

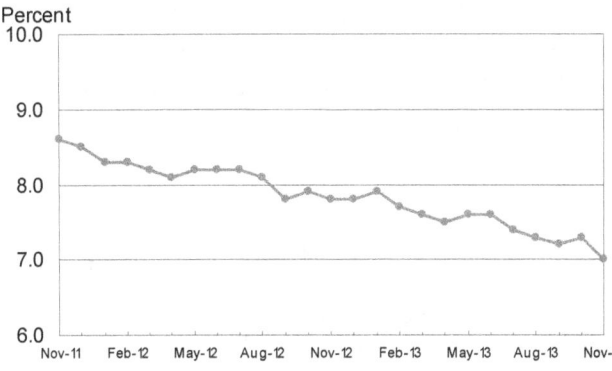

Chart 2. Nonfarm payroll employment over-the-month change, seasonally adjusted, November 2011 – November 2013

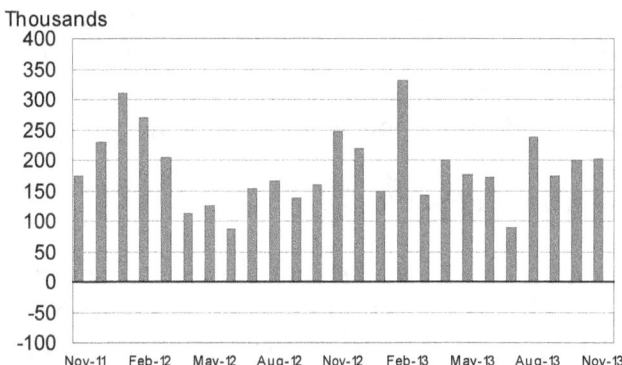

Household Survey Data

Both the number of **unemployed persons**, at 10.9 million, and the **unemployment rate**, at 7.0 percent, declined in November. Among the unemployed, the number who reported being on **temporary layoff** decreased by 377,000. This largely reflects the return to work of federal employees who were furloughed in October due to the partial government shutdown. (See tables A-1 and A-11.)

Among the **major worker groups**, the unemployment rates for adult men (6.7 percent), adult women (6.2 percent), teenagers (20.8 percent), whites (6.2 percent), blacks (12.5 percent), and Hispanics (8.7 percent) changed little in November. The jobless rate for Asians was 5.3 percent (not seasonally adjusted), little changed from a year earlier. (See tables A-1, A-2, and A-3.)

The number of persons **unemployed less than 5 weeks** declined by 300,000 in November, partially reflecting the return to work of federal employees on furlough in October. The number of **long-term**

unemployed (those jobless for 27 weeks or more) was essentially unchanged at 4.1 million in November. These individuals accounted for 37.3 percent of the unemployed. The number of long-term unemployed has declined by 718,000 over the past 12 months. (See table A-12.)

The **civilian labor force** rose by 455,000 in November, after declining by 720,000 in October. The **labor force participation rate** changed little (63.0 percent) in November. Total employment as measured by the household survey increased by 818,000 over the month, following a decline of 735,000 in the prior month. This over-the-month increase in employment partly reflected the return to work of furloughed federal government employees. The **employment-population ratio** increased by 0.3 percentage point to 58.6 percent in November, reversing a decline of the same size in the prior month. (See table A-1.)

The number of persons employed **part time for economic reasons** (sometimes referred to as involuntary part-time workers) fell by 331,000 to 7.7 million in November. These individuals were working part time because their hours had been cut back or because they were unable to find a full-time job. (See table A-8.)

In November, 2.1 million persons were **marginally attached to the labor force**, down by 409,000 from a year earlier. (The data are not seasonally adjusted.) These individuals were not in the labor force, wanted and were available for work, and had looked for a job sometime in the prior 12 months. They were not counted as unemployed because they had not searched for work in the 4 weeks preceding the survey. (See table A-16.)

Among the marginally attached, there were 762,000 **discouraged workers** in November, down by 217,000 from a year ago. (The data are not seasonally adjusted.) Discouraged workers are persons not currently looking for work because they believe no jobs are available for them. The remaining 1.3 million persons marginally attached to the labor force in November had not searched for work for reasons such as school attendance or family responsibilities. (See table A-16.)

Establishment Survey Data

Total **nonfarm payroll employment** increased by 203,000 in November. Job growth averaged 195,000 per month over the prior 12 months. In November, job gains occurred in transportation and warehousing, health care, and manufacturing. (See table B-1.)

Employment in **transportation and warehousing** rose by 31,000 in November, with gains in couriers and messengers (+9,000), truck transportation (+8,000), warehousing and storage (+5,000), and air transportation (+3,000).

Health care employment continued to increase over the month (+28,000). Job gains occurred in home healthcare services (+12,000) and offices of physicians (+7,000), while nursing care facilities lost jobs (-4,000). Job growth in health care has averaged 19,000 per month thus far this year, compared with an average monthly gain of 27,000 in 2012.

In November, **manufacturing** added 27,000 jobs. Within the industry, job gains occurred in food manufacturing (+8,000) and in motor vehicles and parts (+7,000).

In November, employment in **professional and business services** continued to trend up (+35,000). Over the prior 12 months, the industry added an average of 55,000 jobs per month.

Retail trade employment also continued to expand in November (+22,000). Within the industry, job growth occurred in general merchandise stores (+14,000); in sporting goods, hobby, book, and music stores (+12,000); and in automobile dealers (+7,000). Over the prior 12 months, job growth in retail trade averaged 31,000 per month.

Within leisure and hospitality, employment in **food services and drinking places** continued to trend up in November (+18,000). Job growth in this industry averaged 28,000 per month over the prior 12 months.

Employment in **construction** continued to trend up in November (+17,000). Monthly job gains in the industry averaged 15,000 over the prior 12 months.

Federal government employment continued to decline (-7,000) in November. Over the past 12 months, federal government employment has decreased by 92,000.

Employment in other major industries, including **mining and logging, wholesale trade, information, and financial activities**, showed little or no change in November.

The **average workweek for all employees** on private nonfarm payrolls edged up by 0.1 hour to 34.5 hours in November. The manufacturing workweek edged up by 0.1 hour to 41.0 hours, and factory overtime edged up by 0.1 hour to 3.5 hours. The average workweek for **production and nonsupervisory employees** on private nonfarm payrolls edged up by 0.1 hour to 33.7 hours. (See tables B-2 and B-7.)

In November, **average hourly earnings for all employees** on private nonfarm payrolls rose by 4 cents to $24.15. Over the year, average hourly earnings have risen by 48 cents, or 2.0 percent. In November, average hourly earnings of **production and nonsupervisory employees** increased by 3 cents to $20.31. (See tables B-3 and B-8.)

The change in total nonfarm payroll employment for September was revised from +163,000 to +175,000, and the change for October was revised from +204,000 to +200,000. With these revisions, employment gains in September and October combined were 8,000 higher than previously reported.

The Employment Situation for December is scheduled to be released on Friday, January 10, 2014, at 8:30 a.m. (EST).

Household Survey Reference Period

In the household survey, the reference period for November 2013 was the calendar week that included the 5th of the month. Typically, the reference period for the household survey is the calendar week that includes the 12th of the month. The November reference week was moved up in 2013 due to the timing of the November and December holidays. In accordance with usual practice, this change is made in November when necessary to allow for sufficient time to process data and conduct survey operations.

Revision of Seasonally Adjusted Household Survey Data

In accordance with usual practice, The Employment Situation release for December 2013, scheduled for January 10, 2014, will incorporate annual revisions in seasonally adjusted unemployment and other labor force series from the household survey. Seasonally adjusted data for the most recent 5 years are subject to revision.

Upcoming Change to the Household Survey Tables

Effective with the release of January 2014 data on February 7, 2014, household survey table A-10 will include two new seasonally adjusted series for women age 55 and over—the number of unemployed persons and the unemployment rate. These will replace the series that are currently displayed for this group, which are not seasonally adjusted.

HOUSEHOLD DATA
Summary table A. Household data, seasonally adjusted
[Numbers in thousands]

Category	Nov. 2012	Sept. 2013	Oct. 2013	Nov. 2013	Change from: Oct. 2013- Nov. 2013
Employment status					
Civilian noninstitutional population.............................	244,174	246,168	246,381	246,567	186
Civilian labor force..	155,319	155,559	154,839	155,294	455
Participation rate.....................................	63.6	63.2	62.8	63.0	0.2
Employed...	143,277	144,303	143,568	144,386	818
Employment-population ratio...........................	58.7	58.6	58.3	58.6	0.3
Unemployed...	12,042	11,255	11,272	10,907	-365
Unemployment rate...................................	7.8	7.2	7.3	7.0	-0.3
Not in labor force...	88,855	90,609	91,541	91,273	-268
Unemployment rates					
Total, 16 years and over....................................	7.8	7.2	7.3	7.0	-0.3
Adult men (20 years and over)...........................	7.2	7.1	7.0	6.7	-0.3
Adult women (20 years and over).........................	7.0	6.2	6.4	6.2	-0.2
Teenagers (16 to 19 years).............................	23.6	21.4	22.2	20.8	-1.4
White..	6.8	6.3	6.3	6.2	-0.1
Black or African American.............................	13.2	12.9	13.1	12.5	-0.6
Asian (not seasonally adjusted).......................	6.4	5.3	5.2	5.3	–
Hispanic or Latino ethnicity..........................	9.9	9.0	9.1	8.7	-0.4
Total, 25 years and over....................................	6.5	6.0	6.1	5.9	-0.2
Less than a high school diploma........................	12.1	10.3	10.9	10.8	-0.1
High school graduates, no college......................	8.1	7.6	7.3	·7.3	0.0
Some college or associate degree.......................	6.6	6.0	6.3	6.4	0.1
Bachelor's degree and higher...........................	3.9	3.7	3.8	3.4	-0.4
Reason for unemployment					
Job losers and persons who completed temporary jobs.................	6,429	5,844	6,253	5,804	-449
Job leavers...	926	989	861	893	32
Reentrants..	3,325	3,181	3,117	3,073	-44
New entrants..	1,326	1,222	1,223	1,165	-58
Duration of unemployment					
Less than 5 weeks...	2,596	2,596	2,761	2,461	-300
5 to 14 weeks...	2,757	2,703	2,656	2,597	-59
15 to 26 weeks..	1,820	1,804	1,782	1,766	-16
27 weeks and over..	4,784	4,146	4,063	4,066	3
Employed persons at work part time					
Part time for economic reasons............................	8,138	7,926	8,050	7,719	-331
Slack work or business conditions......................	5,084	4,960	5,047	4,869	-178
Could only fin part-time work........................	2,648	2,557	2,599	2,486	-113
Part time for noneconomic reasons.........................	18,594	18,967	18,786	18,876	90
Persons not in the labor force (not seasonally adjusted)					
Marginally attached to the labor force......................	2,505	2,302	2,283	2,096	–
Discouraged workers....................................	979	852	815	762	–

- Over-the-month changes are not displayed for not seasonally adjusted data.

NOTE: Persons whose ethnicity is identifie as Hispanic or Latino may be of any race. Detail for the seasonally adjusted data shown in this table will not necessarily add to totals because of the independent seasonal adjustment of the various series. Updated population controls are introduced annually with the release of January data.

ESTABLISHMENT DATA
Summary table B. Establishment data, seasonally adjusted

Category	Nov. 2012	Sept. 2013	Oct. 2013[p]	Nov. 2013[p]
EMPLOYMENT BY SELECTED INDUSTRY (Over-the-month change, in thousands)				
Total nonfarm.	247	175	200	203
Total private.	256	168	214	196
Goods-producing.	43	29	31	44
Mining and logging.	12	4	3	0
Construction.	24	17	12	17
Manufacturing.	7	8	16	27
Durable goods[1].	17	12	11	17
Motor vehicles and parts.	9.7	2.5	4.1	6.7
Nondurable goods.	-10	-4	5	10
Private service-providing[1].	213	139	183	152
Wholesale trade.	9.8	15.7	-8.1	6.8
Retail trade.	69.6	23.3	45.8	22.3
Transportation and warehousing.	20.2	36.9	3.1	30.5
Informa ion.	14	2	4	-1
Financial ac ivities.	5	-3	7	-3
Professional and business services[1].	55	47	48	35
Temporary help services.	26.5	27.4	9.1	16.4
Education and health services[1].	14	14	30	40
Health care and social assistance.	30.2	19.7	21.3	29.6
Leisure and hospitality.	21	-1	49	17
Other services.	7	4	4	4
Government.	-9	7	-14	7
WOMEN AND PRODUCTION AND NONSUPERVISORY EMPLOYEES AS A PERCENT OF ALL EMPLOYEES[2]				
Total nonfarm women employees.	49.4	49.4	49.4	49.4
Total private women employees.	47.9	47.9	47.9	47.9
Total private production and nonsupervisory employees.	82.6	82.6	82.6	82.6
HOURS AND EARNINGS ALL EMPLOYEES Total private				
Average weekly hours.	34.4	34.4	34.4	34.5
Average hourly earnings.	$23.67	$24.09	$24.11	$24.15
Average weekly earnings.	$814.25	$828.70	$829.38	$833.18
Index of aggregate weekly hours (2007=100)[3].	97.0	98.7	98.8	99.3
Over-the-month percent change.	0.5	-0.1	0.1	0.5
Index of aggregate weekly payrolls (2007=100)[4].	109 5	113.3	113.6	114.4
Over-the-month percent change.	0.9	0.0	0.3	0.7
HOURS AND EARNINGS PRODUCTION AND NONSUPERVISORY EMPLOYEES Total private				
Average weekly hours.	33.7	33.7	33.6	33.7
Average hourly earnings.	$19.88	$20.25	$20.28	$20.31
Average weekly earnings.	$669.96	$682.43	$681.41	$684.45
Index of aggregate weekly hours (2002=100)[3].	104.7	106.3	106.2	106.7
Over-the-month percent change.	0.5	0.1	-0.1	0.5
Index of aggregate weekly payrolls (2002=100)[4].	138 9	143.8	143.9	144.8
Over-the-month percent change.	0.7	0.3	0.1	0.6
DIFFUSION INDEX (Over 1-month span)[5]				
Total private (266 industries).	63.9	61.3	61.1	63.5
Manufacturing (81 industries).	52.5	54.3	56.8	63.0

[1] Includes other industries, not shown separately.

[2] Data relate to production employees in mining and logging and manufacturing, construction employees in construction, and nonsupervisory employees in the service-providing industries.

[3] The indexes of aggregate weekly hours are calculated by dividing the current month's estimates of aggregate hours by the corresponding annual average aggregate hours.

[4] The indexes of aggregate weekly payrolls are calculated by dividing the current month's estimates of aggregate weekly payrolls by the corresponding annual average aggregate weekly payrolls.

[5] Figures are the percent of industries with employment increasing plus one-half of the industries with unchanged employment, where 50 percent indicates an equal balance between industries with increasing and decreasing employment.

p Preliminary

ESTABLISHMENT DATA

Table B-1. Employees on nonfarm payrolls by industry sector and selected industry detail
[In thousands]

Industry	Not seasonally adjusted				Seasonally adjusted				
	Nov. 2012	Sept. 2013	Oct. 2013[p]	Nov. 2013[p]	Nov. 2012	Sept. 2013	Oct. 2013[p]	Nov. 2013[p]	Change from: Oct.2013 - Nov.2013[p]
Total nonfarm.............................	135,636	136,612	137,521	137,942	134,472	136,362	136,562	136,765	203
Total private.............................	113,284	114,871	115,313	115,622	112,593	114,498	114,712	114,908	196
Goods-producing.........................	18,571	18,984	18,972	18,861	18,464	18,674	18,705	18,749	44
Mining and logging..........................	853	894	895	884	853	881	884	884	0
Logging..............................	51.7	54.5	54.2	55.8	50.7	51.7	52.1	54.3	2.2
Mining...............................	800.8	839.1	840.7	828.6	802.0	829.0	831.9	829.6	-2.3
Oil and gas extraction.................	188 8	197.8	198.2	198.4	190.0	197.4	198.6	199.2	0.6
Mining, except oil and gas[1].................	221.7	226.3	226.0	222.4	221.6	221.6	222.4	222.6	0.2
Coal mining.......................	82.5	85.4	85.6	84.5	83.0	85.6	85.9	85.6	-0.3
Support activities for mining...............	390.3	415.0	416.5	407.8	390.4	410.0	410.9	407.8	-3.1
Construction.............................	5,779	6,053	6,052	5,955	5,673	5,822	5,834	5,851	17
Construction of buildings......................	1,263.0	1,303.8	1,315.2	1,302.6	1,241.4	1,273.0	1,279.0	1,282.6	3.6
Residential building....................	584.2	605.1	610.8	605.8	574.2	588.7	594.2	595.5	1.3
Nonresidential building....................	678.8	698.7	704.4	696.8	667.2	684.3	684.8	687.1	2.3
Heavy and civil engineering construction......	908.7	963.8	960.4	925.2	880.2	894.8	895.6	895.8	0.2
Specialty trade contractors....................	3,606.9	3,785.1	3,776.2	3,726.7	3,551.4	3,654.1	3,659.6	3,672.1	12.5
Residential specialty trade contractors......	1,512.5	1,623.5	1,615.9	1,592.3	1,489.8	1,562.5	1,563.9	1,571.0	7.1
Nonresidential specialty trade contractors. ..	2,094.4	2,161.6	2,160.3	2,134.4	2,061.6	2,091.6	2,095.7	2,101.1	5.4
Manufacturing.............................	11,939	12,037	12,025	12,022	11,938	11,971	11,987	12,014	27
Durable goods.............................	7,479	7,545	7,549	7,560	7,483	7,532	7,543	7,560	17
Wood products..........................	342.5	352.7	354.7	354.0	343.5	350.2	353.2	353.8	0.6
Nonmetallic mineral products..............	364.7	376.9	376.9	375.9	362.1	370.9	371.2	373.2	2.0
Primary metals..........................	398.9	394.2	392.4	393.3	399.3	393.0	392.4	394.1	1.7
Fabricated metal products................	1,423.7	1,446.1	1,449.9	1,450.7	1,423.2	1,443.4	1,446.6	1,449.7	3.1
Machinery.............................	1,096.6	1,103.4	1,103.9	1,103.9	1,098.2	1,105 2	1,104.8	1,105.1	0.3
Computer and electronic products[1]..........	1,083.2	1,082.1	1,078.3	1,077.8	1,085.3	1,082.6	1,079.9	1,080.4	0.5
Computer and peripheral equipment......	158.2	164.4	163.5	164.2	158.5	164.5	164.0	164.8	0.8
Communications equipment..............	108.3	104.9	104.4	104.4	108.1	105.1	104.7	104.4	-0.3
Semiconductors and electronic components............................	380.0	379.3	377.0	377.7	381.1	379.0	377.5	378.6	1.1
Electronic instruments.....................	395.8	394.5	394.4	392.5	397.2	394 9	394.8	394.2	-0.6
Electrical equipment and appliances........	368.9	363.8	364.2	364.6	369.9	363.9	364.6	365.2	0.6
Transportation equipment[1].................	1,473.2	1,493.9	1,494.3	1,502.3	1,472.9	1,492.6	1,496.4	1,501.3	4.9
Motor vehicles and parts[2].................	784.5	817.7	819.3	826.9	784.6	815.9	820.0	826.7	6.7
Furniture and related products.............	346.9	354.6	356.1	355.9	349.6	352.7	356.6	358.7	2.1
Miscellaneous durable goods manufacturing..........................	580.6	577.4	578.1	581.4	578.7	577.1	577.5	578.5	1.0
Nondurable goods.............................	4,460	4,492	4,476	4,462	4,455	4,439	4,444	4,454	10
Food manufacturing.......................	1,474.2	1,502.4	1,491.2	1,483.4	1,466.8	1,465.1	1,466.9	1,474.7	7.8
Textile mills...........................	117.3	114.4	115.0	115.5	117.1	113.9	115.0	114.9	-0.1
Textile product mills......................	117.2	114.4	113.9	114.3	117.3	114.4	113.8	113.9	0.1
Apparel..............................	147 5	141.1	140.8	140.8	147.8	140.6	140.5	140.3	-0.2
Paper and paper products.................	376.7	374.4	373.6	373.8	376.8	374.2	373.8	374.3	0.5
Printing and related support activities.......	457.7	444.3	445.1	445.2	457.2	444.2	444.2	444.3	0.1
Petroleum and coal products..............	115.1	116.9	116.7	115.8	114.7	115 0	113.5	115.1	1.6
Chemicals.............................	782.7	791.8	791.5	793.1	785.7	791.9	793.5	795.7	2.2
Plastics and rubber products..............	648.1	659.2	654.9	655.6	648.9	655 2	655.8	657.1	1.3
Miscellaneous nondurable goods manufacturing..........................	223.2	233.3	233.0	224.4	222.7	224.9	227.1	224.1	-3.0
Private service-providing...........................	94,713	95,887	96,341	96,761	94,129	95,824	96,007	96,159	152
Trade, transportation, and utilities................	26,208	26,018	26,184	26,731	25,720	26,101	26,142	26,202	60
Wholesale trade.............................	5,719.8	5,793.8	5,795.4	5,802.0	5,708.8	5,790.9	5,782.8	5,789.6	6.8
Durable goods..........................	2,839.2	2,881.1	2,881.4	2,881.9	2,839.5	2,879.6	2,879.1	2,882.0	2.9
Nondurable goods.......................	1,996.7	2,014.5	2,013.9	2,016.8	1,988.9	2,013 3	2,005.8	2,007.5	1.7
Electronic markets and agents and brokers...............................	883 9	898.2	900.1	903.3	880.4	898 0	897.9	900.1	2.2
Retail trade.............................	15,430.3	15,144.1	15,302.1	15,773.1	14,997.9	15,252.4	15,298.2	15,320.5	22.3
Motor vehicle and parts dealers[1]............	1,745.3	1,800.1	1,795.9	1,797.4	1,748.1	1,787.7	1,790.0	1,798.7	8.7
Automobile dealers........................	1,101.8	1,137.6	1,135.1	1,138.2	1,102.3	1,131.4	1,131.9	1,138.4	6.5

See footnotes at end of table.

Table B-1. Employees on nonfarm payrolls by industry sector and selected industry detail — Continued

[In thousands]

Industry	Not seasonally adjusted				Seasonally adjusted				Change from: Oct.2013 - Nov.2013[P]
	Nov. 2012	Sept. 2013	Oct. 2013[P]	Nov. 2013[P]	Nov. 2012	Sept. 2013	Oct. 2013[P]	Nov. 2013[P]	
Retail trade - Continued									
Furniture and home furnishings stores......	465.1	443.1	457.1	472.6	445.7	450.9	452.2	453.0	0.8
Electronics and appliance stores...........	541.3	506.7	530.8	557.8	513.8	517.8	527.9	524.3	-3.6
Building material and garden supply stores...................................	1,143.8	1,189.6	1,189.8	1,185.9	1,174 0	1,203.2	1,210.4	1,213.9	3.5
Food and beverage stores.................	2,904.3	2,943.0	2,961.9	2,976.8	2,879.6	2,945.2	2,956.2	2,950.8	-5.4
Health and personal care stores...........	1,030.5	1,034.0	1,040.2	1,051.3	1,017.3	1,039.1	1,040.7	1,037.3	-3.4
Gasoline stations........................	846.4	867.8	869.0	871.4	844.3	863.0	867.3	868.1	0.8
Clothing and clothing accessories stores....	1,598.3	1,416.2	1,427.6	1,571.1	1,460.1	1,442.1	1,430.8	1,432.8	2.0
Sporting goods, hobby, book, and music stores...................................	617.2	584.8	596.0	654.3	578 3	587.8	597.9	609.6	11.7
General merchandise stores[1].............	3,243.5	3,099.3	3,147.8	3,338.0	3,090.3	3,157.8	3,165.2	3,179.0	13.8
Department stores.....................	1,587.2	1,454.3	1,480.0	1,611.8	1,479.3	1,497.4	1,499.0	1,503.3	4.3
Miscellaneous store retailers..............	823.2	811.2	817.6	815.9	807.8	806.9	805.6	803.5	-2.1
Nonstore retailers.......................	471.4	448.3	468.4	480.6	438.6	450.9	454.0	449.5	-4.5
Transportation and warehousing..............	4,505.7	4,524.3	4,530.7	4,600.7	4,459.0	4,501.0	4,504.1	4,534.6	30.5
Air transportation.......................	451.2	445.9	444.5	446.3	454.8	445.6	446.4	449.8	3.4
Rail transportation......................	230.2	230.0	230.0	230.0	230.0	230.2	229.9	229.9	0.0
Water transportation....................	62.6	63.6	63.1	62.8	63.6	62.5	62.6	63.5	0.9
Truck transportation.....................	1,376.7	1,405.8	1,403.0	1,405.2	1,366.7	1,386.1	1,386.9	1,395.3	8.4
Transit and ground passenger transportation.........................	474.9	484.3	490.1	493.7	458.0	473.5	472.0	476.0	4.0
Pipeline transportation...................	43.7	45.3	45.4	45.4	44.0	45.2	45.4	45.6	0.2
Scenic and sightseeing transportation.......	24.2	30.7	26.0	22.0	26.6	25.7	25.3	24.8	-0.5
Support activi ies for transportation..........	585.0	590.9	592.2	593.3	583.1	592.0	589.7	590.6	0.9
Couriers and messengers..................	550.9	524.4	526.7	579.9	536.8	540.6	544.8	553.4	8.6
Warehousing and storage..................	706.3	703.4	709.7	722.1	695.4	699.6	701.1	705.7	4.6
Utilities...............................	552.6	555.4	555.8	555.5	554.7	556.4	556.6	557.5	0.9
Informa ion.............................	2,693	2,665	2,674	2,692	2,685	2,681	2,685	2,684	-1
Publishing industries, except Internet...........	735.5	727.3	727.4	728.8	732.7	726.1	725.4	726.1	0.7
Mo ion picture and sound recording industries.............................	389.1	354.7	356.5	374.5	386.0	368.7	370.6	371.0	0.4
Broadcasting, except Internet...............	285.5	287.1	288.7	289.3	284.3	286.6	287.9	288.0	0.1
Telecommunications......................	854.9	857.4	858.6	856.9	854.1	859.8	858.9	856.8	-2.1
Data processing, hosting and related services...............................	250.7	253.8	254.5	255.0	249.9	255.0	254.8	254.6	-0.2
Other information services..................	177.7	184.4	188.0	187.6	177.8	185.1	187.7	187.7	0.0
Financial ac ivities.........................	7,821	7,904	7,911	7,900	7,822	7,901	7,908	7,905	-3
Finance and insurance.....................	5,871.5	5,893.3	5,903.7	5,905.7	5,865 2	5,903.2	5,905.5	5,900.2	-5 3
Monetary authorities - central bank..........	17.3	16.8	16.9	17.3	17.3	16.8	16.8	17.1	0.3
Credit intermediation and related activities[1]............................	2,601.6	2,595.7	2,591.1	2,585.2	2,599.2	2,598.6	2,594.4	2,585.0	-9.4
Depository credit intermedia ion[1]..........	1,738.7	1,720.0	1,717.8	1,715.0	1,741.2	1,724.7	1,722.2	1,718.5	-3.7
Commercial banking....................	1,315.7	1,289.7	1,288.0	1,284.1	1,318.6	1,293.5	1,290.6	1,287.5	-3.1
Securities, commodity contracts, investments............................	817.2	828.1	834.0	833.0	814.4	831.4	832.6	830.9	-1.7
Insurance carriers and related activities.....	2,348.2	2,366.6	2,375.0	2,383.3	2,347.2	2,369.9	2,374.9	2,380.5	5.6
Funds, trusts, and other financia vehicles...	87.2	86.1	86.7	86.9	87.1	86.5	86.8	86.7	-0.1
Real estate and rental and leasing............	1,949.0	2,010.2	2,007.3	1,994.5	1,956.9	1,998.0	2,002.3	2,004.4	2.1
Real estate.............................	1,415.7	1,457.4	1,458.4	1,448.4	1,419.6	1,450.6	1,454.3	1,453.6	-0.7
Rental and leasing services................	509.3	529.9	526.4	523.5	513.6	524.6	525.5	528.4	2.9
Lessors of nonfinancia intangible assets....	24.0	22.9	22.5	22.6	23.7	22.8	22.5	22.4	-0.1
Professional and business services..............	18,266	18,755	18,893	18,892	18,117	18,677	18,725	18,760	35
Professional and technical services[1]..........	7,966.3	8,066.5	8,143.4	8,175.3	7,977.4	8,153.2	8,174.8	8,192.3	17.5
Legal services...........................	1,127.9	1,124.2	1,131.3	1,130.5	1,126.1	1,130.1	1,129.7	1,128.6	-1.1
Accounting and bookkeeping services......	866.1	869.8	880.2	904.2	911.7	947.4	951.1	956.6	5.5
Architectural and engineering services......	1,335.2	1,365.7	1,370.8	1,366.3	1,332.1	1,358.5	1,362.7	1,363.7	1.0
Computer systems design and related services...............................	1,662.1	1,693.2	1,712.4	1,715.5	1,655 2	1,698.8	1,705.9	1,708.6	2.7
Management and technical consulting services...............................	1,152.9	1,193.7	1,212.4	1,212.7	1,141 8	1,195.2	1,201.7	1,202.3	0.6

See footnotes at end of table.

Frequently Asked Questions about Employment and Unemployment Estimates

1. Why are there two monthly measures of employment?

The household survey and establishment survey both produce sample-based estimates of employment, and both have strengths and limitations. The establishment survey employment series has a smaller margin of error on the measurement of month-to-month change than the household survey because of its much larger sample size. An over-the-month employment change of about 100,000 is statistically significant in the establishment survey, while the threshold for a statistically significant change in the household survey is about 400,000. However, the household survey has a more expansive scope than the establishment survey because it includes self-employed workers whose businesses are unincorporated, unpaid family workers, agricultural workers, and private household workers, who are excluded by the establishment survey. The household survey also provides estimates of employment for demographic groups. For more information on the differences between the two surveys, please visit www.bls.gov/web/empsit/ces cps trends.pdf.

2. Are undocumented immigrants counted in the surveys?

It is likely that both surveys include at least some undocumented immigrants. However, neither the establishment nor the household survey is designed to identify the legal status of workers. Therefore, it is not possible to determine how many are counted in either survey. The establishment survey does not collect data on the legal status of workers. The household survey does include questions which identify the foreign and native born, but it does not include questions about the legal status of the foreign born. Data on the foreign and native born are published each month in table A-7 of The Employment Situation news release.

3. Why does the establishment survey have revisions?

The establishment survey revises published estimates to improve its data series by incorporating additional information that was not available at the time of the initial publication of the estimates. The establishment survey revises its initial monthly estimates twice, in the immediately succeeding 2 months, to incorporate additional sample receipts from respondents in the survey and recalculated seasonal adjustment factors. For more information on the monthly revisions, please visit www.bls.gov/ces/cesrevinfo.htm.

On an annual basis, the establishment survey incorporates a benchmark revision that re-anchors estimates to nearly complete employment counts available from unemployment insurance tax records. The benchmark helps to control for sampling and modeling errors in the estimates. For more information on the annual benchmark revision, please visit www.bls.gov/web/empsit/cesbmart.htm.

4. Does the establishment survey sample include small firms?

Yes; about 40 percent of the establishment survey sample is comprised of business establishments with fewer than 20 employees. The establishment survey sample is designed to maximize the reliability of the statewide total nonfarm employment estimate; firms from all states, size classes, and industries are appropriately sampled to achieve that goal.

5. Does the establishment survey account for employment from new businesses?

Yes; monthly establishment survey estimates include an adjustment to account for the net employment change generated by business births and deaths. The adjustment comes from an econometric model that forecasts the monthly net jobs impact of business births and deaths based on the actual past values of the net impact that can be observed with a lag from the Quarterly Census of Employment and Wages. The establishment survey uses modeling rather than sampling for this purpose because the survey is not immediately able to bring new businesses into the sample. There is an unavoidable lag between the birth of a new firm and its appearance on the sampling frame and availability for selection. BLS adds new businesses to the survey twice a year.

6. Is the count of unemployed persons limited to just those people receiving unemployment insurance benefits?

No; the estimate of unemployment is based on a monthly sample survey of households. All persons who are without jobs and are actively seeking and available to work are included among the unemployed. (People on temporary layoff are included even if they do not actively seek work.) There is no requirement or question relating to unemployment insurance benefits in the monthly survey.

7. Does the official unemployment rate exclude people who want a job but are not currently looking for work?

Yes; however, there are separate estimates of persons outside the labor force who want a job, including those who are not currently looking because they believe no jobs are available (discouraged workers). In addition, alternative measures of labor underutilization (some of which include discouraged workers and other groups not officially counted as unemployed) are published each month in table A-15 of The Employment Situation news release. For more information about these alternative measures, please visit www.bls.gov/cps/lfcharacteristics.htm#altmeasures.

8. How can unusually severe weather affect employment and hours estimates?

In the establishment survey, the reference period is the pay period that includes the 12th of the month. Unusually severe weather is more likely to have an impact on average weekly hours than on employment. Average weekly hours are estimated for paid time during the pay period, including pay for holidays, sick leave, or other time off. The impact of severe weather on hours estimates typically, but not always, results in a reduction in average weekly hours. For example, some employees may be off work for part of the pay period and not receive pay for the time missed, while some workers, such as those dealing with cleanup or repair, may work extra hours.

In order for severe weather conditions to reduce the estimate of payroll employment, employees have to be off work without pay for the entire pay period. Slightly more than 20 percent of all employees in the payroll survey sample have a weekly pay period. Employees who receive pay for any part of the pay period, even 1 hour, are counted in the payroll employment figures. It is not possible to quantify the effect of extreme weather on estimates of over-the-month change in employment.

In the household survey, the reference period is generally the calendar week that includes the 12th of the month. Persons who miss the entire week's work for weather-related events are counted as employed whether or not they are paid for the time off. The household survey collects data on the number of persons who had a job but were not at work due to bad weather. It also provides a measure of the number of persons who usually work full time but had reduced hours. Current and historical data are available on the household survey's most requested statistics page at http://data.bls.gov/cgi-bin/surveymost?ln.

Technical Note

This news release presents statistics from two major surveys, the Current Population Survey (CPS; household survey) and the Current Employment Statistics survey (CES; establishment survey). The household survey provides information on the labor force, employment, and unemployment that appears in the "A" tables, marked HOUSEHOLD DATA. It is a sample survey of about 60,000 eligible households conducted by the U.S. Census Bureau for the U.S. Bureau of Labor Statistics (BLS).

The establishment survey provides information on employment, hours, and earnings of employees on nonfarm payrolls; the data appear in the "B" tables, marked ESTABLISHMENT DATA. BLS collects these data each month from the payroll records of a sample of nonagricultural business establishments. Each month the CES program surveys about 145,000 businesses and government agencies, representing approximately 557,000 individual worksites, in order to provide detailed industry data on employment, hours, and earnings of workers on nonfarm payrolls. The active sample includes approximately one-third of all nonfarm payroll employees.

For both surveys, the data for a given month relate to a particular week or pay period. In the household survey, the reference period is generally the calendar week that contains the 12th day of the month. In the establishment survey, the reference period is the pay period including the 12th, which may or may not correspond directly to the calendar week.

Coverage, definitions, and differences between surveys

Household survey. The sample is selected to reflect the entire civilian noninstitutional population. Based on responses to a series of questions on work and job search activities, each person 16 years and over in a sample household is classified as employed, unemployed, or not in the labor force.

People are classified as *employed* if they did any work at all as paid employees during the reference week; worked in their own business, profession, or on their own farm; or worked without pay at least 15 hours in a family business or farm. People are also counted as employed if they were temporarily absent from their jobs because of illness, bad weather, vacation, labor-management disputes, or personal reasons.

People are classified as *unemployed* if they meet all of the following criteria: they had no employment during the reference week; they were available for work at that time; and they made specific efforts to find employment sometime during the 4-week period ending with the reference week. Persons laid off from a job and expecting recall need not be looking for work to be counted as unemployed. The unemployment data derived from the household survey in no way depend upon the eligibility for or receipt of unemployment insurance benefits.

The *civilian labor force* is the sum of employed and unemployed persons. Those persons not classified as employed or unemployed are *not in the labor force*. The *unemployment rate* is the number unemployed as a percent of the labor force. The *labor force participation rate* is the labor force as a percent of the population, and the *employment-population ratio* is the employed as a percent of the population. Additional information about the household survey can be found at www.bls.gov/cps/documentation.htm.

Establishment survey. The sample establishments are drawn from private nonfarm businesses such as factories, offices, and stores, as well as from federal, state, and local government entities. *Employees on nonfarm payrolls* are those who received pay for any part of the reference pay period, including persons on paid leave. Persons are counted in each job they hold. *Hours and earnings* data are produced for the private sector for all employees and for production and nonsupervisory employees. *Production and nonsupervisory* employees are defined as production and related employees in manufacturing and mining and logging, construction workers in construction, and non-supervisory employees in private service-providing industries.

Industries are classified on the basis of an establishment's principal activity in accordance with the 2012 version of the North American Industry Classification System. Additional information about the establishment survey can be found at www.bls.gov/ces/.

Differences in employment estimates. The numerous conceptual and methodological differences between the household and establishment surveys result in important distinctions in the employment estimates derived from the surveys. Among these are:

- The household survey includes agricultural workers, self-employed workers whose businesses are unicorporated, unpaid family workers, and private household workers among the employed. These groups are excluded from the establishment survey.

- The household survey includes people on unpaid leave among the employed. The establishment survey does not.

- The household survey is limited to workers 16 years of age and older. The establishment survey is not limited by age.

- The household survey has no duplication of individuals, because individuals are counted only once, even if they hold more than one job. In the establishment survey, employees working at more than one job and thus appearing on more than one payroll are counted separately for each appearance.

Seasonal adjustment

Over the course of a year, the size of the nation's labor force and the levels of employment and unemployment undergo regularly occurring fluctuations. These events may result from seasonal changes in weather, major holidays, and the opening and closing of schools. The effect of such seasonal variation can be very large.

Because these seasonal events follow a more or less regular pattern each year, their influence on the level of a series can be tempered by adjusting for regular seasonal variation. These adjustments make nonseasonal developments, such as declines in employment or increases in the participation of women in the labor force, easier to spot. For example, in the household survey, the large number of youth entering the labor force each June is likely to obscure any other changes that have taken place relative to May, making it difficult to determine if the level of economic activity has risen or declined. Similarly, in the establishment survey, payroll employment in education declines by about 20 percent at the end of the spring term and later rises with the start of the fall term, obscuring the underlying employment trends in the industry. Because seasonal employment changes at the end and beginning of the school year can be estimated, the statistics can be adjusted to make underlying employment patterns more discernable. The seasonally adjusted figures provide a more useful tool with which to analyze changes in month-to-month economic activity.

Many seasonally adjusted series are independently adjusted in both the household and establishment surveys. However, the adjusted series for many major estimates, such as total payroll employment, employment in most major sectors, total employment, and unemployment are computed by aggregating independently adjusted component series. For example, total unemployment is derived by summing the adjusted series for four major age-sex components; this differs from the unemployment estimate that would be obtained by directly adjusting the total or by combining the duration, reasons, or more detailed age categories.

For both the household and establishment surveys, a concurrent seasonal adjustment methodology is used in which new seasonal factors are calculated each month using all relevant data, up to and including the data for the current month. In the household survey, new seasonal factors are used to adjust only the current month's data. In the establishment survey, however, new seasonal factors are used each month to adjust the three most recent monthly estimates. The prior 2 months are routinely revised to incorporate additional sample reports and recalculated seasonal adjustment factors. In both surveys, 5-year revisions to historical data are made once a year.

Reliability of the estimates

Statistics based on the household and establishment surveys are subject to both sampling and nonsampling error. When a sample, rather than the entire population, is surveyed, there is a chance that the sample estimates may differ from the true population values they represent. The component of this difference that occurs because samples differ by chance is known as *sampling error*, and its variability is measured by the standard error of the estimate. There is about a 90-percent chance, or level of confidence, that an estimate based on a sample will differ by no more than 1.6 standard errors from the true population value because of sampling error. BLS analyses are generally conducted at the 90-percent level of confidence.

For example, the confidence interval for the monthly change in total nonfarm employment from the establishment survey is on the order of plus or minus 90,000. Suppose the estimate of nonfarm employment increases by 50,000 from one month to the next. The 90-percent confidence interval on the monthly change would range from -40,000 to +140,000 (50,000 +/- 90,000). These figures do not mean that the sample results are off by these magnitudes, but rather that there is about a 90-percent chance that the true over-the-month change lies within this interval. Since this range includes values of less than zero, we could not say with confidence that nonfarm employment had, in fact, increased that month. If, however, the reported nonfarm employment rise was 250,000, then all of the values within the 90-percent confidence interval would be greater than zero. In this case, it is likely (at least a 90-percent chance) that nonfarm employment had, in fact, risen that month. At an unemployment rate of around 6.0 percent, the 90-percent confidence interval for the monthly change in unemployment as measured by the household survey is about +/- 300,000, and for the monthly change in the unemployment rate it is about +/- 0.2 percentage point.

In general, estimates involving many individuals or establishments have lower standard errors (relative to the size of the estimate) than estimates which are based on a small number of observations. The precision of estimates also is improved when the data are cumulated over time, such as for quarterly and annual averages.

The household and establishment surveys are also affected by *nonsampling error*, which can occur for many reasons, including the failure to sample a segment of the population, inability to obtain information for all respondents in the sample, inability or unwillingness of respondents to provide correct information on a timely basis, mistakes made by respondents, and errors made in the collection or processing of the data.

For example, in the establishment survey, estimates for the most recent 2 months are based on incomplete returns; for this reason, these estimates are labeled preliminary in the tables. It is only after two successive revisions to a monthly estimate, when nearly all sample reports have been received, that the estimate is considered final.

Another major source of nonsampling error in the establishment survey is the inability to capture, on a timely basis, employment generated by new firms. To correct for this systematic underestimation of employment growth, an estimation procedure with two components is used to account for business births. The first component excludes employment losses from business deaths from sample-based estimation in order to offset the missing employment gains from business births. This is incorporated into the sample-based estimation procedure by simply not reflecting sample units going out of business, but imputing to them the same employment trend as the other firms in the sample. This procedure accounts for most of the net birth/death employment.

The second component is an ARIMA time series model designed to estimate the residual net birth/death employment not accounted for by the imputation. The historical time series used to create and test the ARIMA model was derived from the unemployment insurance universe micro-level database, and reflects the actual residual net of births and deaths over the past 5 years.

The sample-based estimates from the establishment survey are adjusted once a year (on a lagged basis) to universe counts of payroll employment obtained from administrative records of the unemployment insurance program. The difference between the March sample-based employment estimates and the March universe counts is known as a benchmark revision, and serves as a rough proxy for total survey error. The new benchmarks also incorporate changes in the classification of industries. Over the past decade, absolute benchmark revisions for total nonfarm employment have averaged 0.3 percent, with a range from -0.7 to 0.6 percent.

Other information

Information in this release will be made available to sensory impaired individuals upon request. Voice phone: (202) 691-5200; Federal Relay Service: (800) 877-8339.

HOUSEHOLD DATA

Table A-1. Employment status of the civilian population by sex and age

[Numbers in thousands]

Employment status, sex, and age	Not seasonally adjusted			Seasonally adjusted[1]					
	Nov. 2012	Oct. 2013	Nov. 2013	Nov. 2012	July 2013	Aug. 2013	Sept. 2013	Oct. 2013	Nov. 2013
TOTAL									
Civilian noninstitutional population	244,174	246,381	246,567	244,174	245,756	245,959	246,168	246,381	246,567
Civilian labor force	154,953	154,918	155,046	155,319	155,798	155,486	155,559	154,839	155,294
Participation rate	63.5	62 9	62.9	63.6	63.4	63.2	63 2	62.8	63.0
Employed	143,549	144,144	144,775	143,277	144,285	144,170	144,303	143,568	144,386
Employment-population ratio	58.8	58.5	58.7	58.7	58.7	58.6	58.6	58.3	58.6
Unemployed	11,404	10,773	10,271	12,042	11,514	11,316	11,255	11,272	10,907
Unemployment rate	7.4	7.0	6.6	7.8	7.4	7.3	7.2	7.3	7.0
Not in labor force	89,221	91,463	91,521	88,855	89,957	90,473	90,609	91,541	91,273
Persons who currently want a job	6,495	5,683	5,437	6,827	6,619	6,285	6,163	6,162	5,754
Men, 16 years and over									
Civilian noninstitutional population	117,810	118,916	119,011	117,810	118,595	118,700	118,807	118,916	119,011
Civilian labor force	82,310	82,261	82,397	82,514	82,852	82,513	82,854	82,347	82,580
Participation rate	69.9	69 2	69.2	70.0	69.9	69.5	69.7	69.2	69.4
Employed	76,142	76,403	76,726	75,983	76,466	76,164	76,452	76,074	76,541
Employment-population ratio	64.6	64.2	64.5	64.5	64.5	64.2	64.4	64.0	64.3
Unemployed	6,167	5,858	5,671	6,530	6,387	6,349	6,401	6,274	6,039
Unemployment rate	7.5	7.1	6.9	7.9	7.7	7.7	7.7	7.6	7.3
Not in labor force	35,501	36,654	36,614	35,297	35,743	36,186	35,953	36,568	36,431
Men, 20 years and over									
Civilian noninstitutional population	109,206	110,414	110,515	109,206	110,054	110,172	110,292	110,414	110,515
Civilian labor force	79,554	79,468	79,743	79,568	79,909	79,639	79,797	79,420	79,741
Participation rate	72.8	72 0	72.2	72.9	72.6	72.3	72.4	71.9	72.2
Employed	74,121	74,290	74,686	73,821	74,328	74,010	74,143	73,869	74,361
Employment-population ratio	67.9	67.3	67.6	67.6	67.5	67.2	67 2	66.9	67.3
Unemployed	5,433	5,178	5,058	5,747	5,581	5,629	5,654	5,551	5,380
Unemployment rate	6.8	6.5	6.3	7.2	7.0	7.1	7.1	7.0	6.7
Not in labor force	29,652	30,947	30,772	29,638	30,145	30,533	30,495	30,994	30,774
Women, 16 years and over									
Civilian noninstitutional population	126,364	127,465	127,555	126,364	127,161	127,260	127,361	127,465	127,555
Civilian labor force	72,644	72,656	72,649	72,806	72,946	72,973	72,705	72,492	72,713
Participation rate	57.5	57 0	57.0	57.6	57.4	57.3	57.1	56.9	57.0
Employed	67,407	67,741	68,049	67,294	67,819	68,005	67,851	67,494	67,845
Employment-population ratio	53.3	53.1	53.3	53.3	53.3	53.4	53 3	53.0	53.2
Unemployed	5,237	4,915	4,600	5,512	5,127	4,968	4,854	4,998	4,868
Unemployment rate	7.2	6.8	6.3	7.6	7.0	6.8	6.7	6.9	6.7
Not in labor force	53,720	54,809	54,907	53,558	54,215	54,287	54,657	54,973	54,842
Women, 20 years and over									
Civilian noninstitutional population	118,079	119,246	119,341	118,079	118,907	119,018	119,131	119,246	119,341
Civilian labor force	69,873	69,968	69,912	69,907	70,033	70,140	69,936	69,707	69,867
Participation rate	59.2	58.7	58.6	59.2	58.9	58.9	58.7	58.5	58.5
Employed	65,175	65,565	65,775	64,988	65,489	65,750	65,582	65,255	65,523
Employment-population ratio	55.2	55.0	55.1	55.0	55.1	55.2	55.1	54.7	54.9
Unemployed	4,698	4,403	4,137	4,918	4,544	4,390	4,354	4,451	4,344
Unemployment rate	6.7	6.3	5.9	7.0	6.5	6.3	6.2	6.4	6.2
Not in labor force	48,206	49,278	49,429	48,172	48,875	48,878	49,195	49,539	49,474
Both sexes, 16 to 19 years									
Civilian noninstitutional population	16,890	16,721	16,710	16,890	16,795	16,770	16,745	16,721	16,710
Civilian labor force	5,526	5,482	5,390	5,845	5,857	5,707	5,825	5,713	5,685
Participation rate	32.7	32 8	32.3	34.6	34.9	34.0	34 8	34.2	34.0
Employed	4,252	4,289	4,315	4,468	4,469	4,410	4,578	4,443	4,502
Employment-population ratio	25.2	25.7	25.8	26.5	26.6	26.3	27 3	26.6	26.9
Unemployed	1,273	1,193	1,076	1,376	1,388	1,297	1,248	1,269	1,183
Unemployment rate	23.0	21.8	20.0	23.6	23.7	22.7	21.4	22.2	20.8
Not in labor force	11,364	11,239	11,320	11,045	10,938	11,062	10,920	11,008	11,025

[1] The population figure are not adjusted for seasonal variation; therefore, identical numbers appear in the unadjusted and seasonally adjusted columns.

NOTE: Updated population controls are introduced annually with the release of January data.

Table A-2. Employment status of the civilian population by race, sex, and age

[Numbers in thousands]

Employment status, race, sex, and age	Not seasonally adjusted			Seasonally adjusted[1]					
	Nov. 2012	Oct. 2013	Nov. 2013	Nov. 2012	July 2013	Aug. 2013	Sept. 2013	Oct. 2013	Nov. 2013
WHITE									
Civilian noninstitutional population..................	193,748	194,734	194,833	193,748	194,373	194,489	194,610	194,734	194,833
Civilian labor force..........................	123,503	122,916	123,123	123,540	123,719	123,378	123,179	122,711	123,031
Participation rate....................	63.7	63.1	63.2	63.8	63.7	63.4	63 3	63.0	63.1
Employed........................	115,571	115,530	116,056	115,124	115,552	115,464	115,388	114,920	115,458
Employment-population ratio..................	59.7	59.3	59.6	59.4	59.4	59.4	59 3	59.0	59.3
Unemployed......................	7,932	7,386	7,067	8,416	8,167	7,913	7,791	7,791	7,573
Unemployment rate...................	6.4	6.0	5.7	6.8	6.6	6.4	6.3	6.3	6.2
Not in labor force............................	70,244	71,818	71,710	70,207	70,654	71,112	71,431	72,023	71,803
Men, 20 years and over									
Civilian labor force..........................	64,607	64,206	64,475	64,509	64,595	64,433	64,323	64,072	64,288
Participation rate....................	73.3	72.4	72.6	73.2	73.0	72.8	72.6	72.2	72.4
Employed........................	60,713	60,537	60,871	60,397	60,528	60,416	60,408	60,128	60,442
Employment-population ratio..................	68.9	68.2	68.6	68.5	68.4	68.2	68.1	67.8	68.1
Unemployed......................	3,894	3,669	3,605	4,112	4,067	4,017	3,915	3,944	3,846
Unemployment rate...................	6.0	5.7	5.6	6.4	6.3	6.2	6.1	6.2	6.0
Women, 20 years and over									
Civilian labor force..........................	54,471	54,295	54,298	54,366	54,501	54,474	54,279	54,061	54,180
Participation rate....................	58.5	58 0	58.0	58.4	58.4	58.3	58.1	57.8	57.9
Employed........................	51,292	51,419	51,596	51,008	51,339	51,494	51,285	51,102	51,304
Employment-population ratio..................	55.1	55.0	55.1	54.8	55.0	55.1	54 8	54.6	54.8
Unemployed......................	3,180	2,875	2,702	3,358	3,162	2,980	2,994	2,959	2,876
Unemployment rate...................	5.8	5.3	5.0	6.2	5.8	5.5	5.5	5.5	5.3
Both sexes, 16 to 19 years									
Civilian labor force..........................	4,425	4,415	4,350	4,665	4,623	4,470	4,577	4,578	4,562
Participation rate....................	35.1	35 5	35.0	37.0	37.0	35.8	36.7	36.8	36.7
Employed........................	3,567	3,574	3,589	3,718	3,685	3,555	3,695	3,690	3,712
Employment-population ratio..................	28.3	28.7	28.8	29.5	29.5	28.5	29.6	29.6	29.8
Unemployed......................	858	842	760	946	938	916	882	888	851
Unemployment rate...................	19.4	19.1	17.5	20.3	20.3	20.5	19.3	19.4	18.6
BLACK OR AFRICAN AMERICAN									
Civilian noninstitutional population....................	30,061	30,500	30,535	30,061	30,390	30,426	30,462	30,500	30,535
Civilian labor force..........................	18,407	18,599	18,460	18,374	18,671	18,511	18,670	18,512	18,506
Participation rate....................	61.2	61 0	60.5	61.1	61.4	60.8	61 3	60.7	60.6
Employed........................	16,065	16,229	16,262	15,952	16,318	16,108	16,269	16,085	16,186
Employment-population ratio..................	53.4	53.2	53.3	53.1	53.7	52.9	53.4	52.7	53.0
Unemployed......................	2,342	2,370	2,199	2,422	2,353	2,403	2,402	2,427	2,320
Unemployment rate...................	12.7	12.7	11.9	13.2	12.6	13.0	12.9	13.1	12.5
Not in labor force............................	11,654	11,901	12,075	11,687	11,719	11,914	11,792	11,988	12,029
Men, 20 years and over									
Civilian labor force..........................	8,275	8,387	8,362	8,225	8,434	8,324	8,499	8,377	8,364
Participation rate....................	67.4	66 9	66.5	66.9	67.6	66.6	67 9	66.8	66.6
Employed........................	7,259	7,364	7,416	7,165	7,382	7,204	7,307	7,289	7,339
Employment-population ratio..................	59.1	58.7	59.0	58.3	59.2	57.6	58 3	58.1	58.4
Unemployed......................	1,016	1,022	945	1,060	1,052	1,120	1,192	1,089	1,025
Unemployment rate...................	12.3	12.2	11.3	12.9	12.5	13.5	14.0	13.0	12.3
Women, 20 years and over									
Civilian labor force..........................	9,464	9,540	9,471	9,444	9,508	9,450	9,421	9,442	9,470
Participation rate....................	62.4	61 9	61.4	62.3	62.0	61.5	61 2	61.3	61.4
Employed........................	8,404	8,419	8,443	8,360	8,510	8,449	8,475	8,353	8,415
Employment-population ratio..................	55.4	54.6	54.7	55.1	55.5	55.0	55.1	54.2	54.5
Unemployed......................	1,060	1,121	1,028	1,085	998	1,001	946	1,089	1,055
Unemployment rate...................	11.2	11.8	10.9	11.5	10.5	10.6	10.0	11.5	11.1
Both sexes, 16 to 19 years									
Civilian labor force..........................	668	672	628	704	729	738	750	693	672
Participation rate....................	25.6	26.4	24.8	27.0	28.4	28.9	29.4	27.3	26.5
Employed........................	402	445	402	427	426	456	487	444	432
Employment-population ratio..................	15.4	17.5	15.9	16.4	16.6	17.8	19.1	17.5	17.0
Unemployed......................	266	227	225	277	303	282	263	249	241
Unemployment rate...................	39.8	33.7	35.9	39.3	41.6	38.2	35.1	36.0	35.8
ASIAN									
Civilian noninstitutional population....................	12,934	13,355	13,484	–	–	–	–	–	–

See footnotes at end of table.

Table A-2. Employment status of the civilian population by race, sex, and age — Continued

[Numbers in thousands]

Employment status, race, sex, and age	Not seasonally adjusted			Seasonally adjusted[1]					
	Nov. 2012	Oct. 2013	Nov. 2013	Nov. 2012	July 2013	Aug. 2013	Sept. 2013	Oct. 2013	Nov. 2013
Civilian labor force.................................	8,344	8,498	8,666	–	–	–	–	–	–
Participation rate.................................	64.5	63.6	64.3	–	–	–	–	–	–
Employed...	7,814	8,055	8,209	–	–	–	–	–	–
Employment-population ratio....................	60.4	60 3	60.9	–	–	–	–	–	–
Unemployed.......................................	530	443	457	–	–	–	–	–	–
Unemployment rate.............................	6.4	5.2	5.3	–	–	–	–	–	–
Not in labor force.................................	4,590	4,857	4,819	–	–	–	–	–	–

[1] The population figure are not adjusted for seasonal variation; therefore, identical numbers appear in the unadjusted and seasonally adjusted columns.

- Data not available.

NOTE: Estimates for the above race groups will not sum to totals shown in table A-1 because data are not presented for all races. Updated population controls are introduced annually with the release of January data.

HOUSEHOLD DATA
Table A-3. Employment status of the Hispanic or Latino population by sex and age
[Numbers in thousands]

Employment status, sex, and age	Not seasonally adjusted			Seasonally adjusted[1]					
	Nov. 2012	Oct. 2013	Nov. 2013	Nov. 2012	July 2013	Aug. 2013	Sept. 2013	Oct. 2013	Nov. 2013
HISPANIC OR LATINO ETHNICITY									
Civilian noninstitutional population...............	37,147	37,796	37,876	37,147	37,548	37,630	37,713	37,796	37,876
Civilian labor force.............................	24,479	24,827	25,060	24,544	25,040	24,942	24,826	24,808	25,109
Participation rate..............................	65.9	65.7	66.2	66.1	66.7	66.3	65.8	65.6	66.3
Employed..	22,086	22,643	22,905	22,109	22,675	22,612	22,598	22,555	22,923
Employment-population ratio..............	59.5	59.9	60.5	59.5	60.4	60.1	59.9	59.7	60.5
Unemployed....................................	2,394	2,184	2,154	2,435	2,366	2,330	2,228	2,253	2,186
Unemployment rate.........................	9.8	8.8	8.6	9.9	9.4	9.3	9.0	9.1	8.7
Not in labor force................................	12,667	12,968	12,817	12,602	12,508	12,688	12,887	12,988	12,767
Men, 20 years and over									
Civilian labor force.............................	13,463	13,790	13,967	–	–	–	–	–	–
Participation rate..............................	80.3	80.8	81.6	–	–	–	–	–	–
Employed..	12,414	12,715	12,896	–	–	–	–	–	–
Employment-population ratio..............	74.1	74.5	75.4	–	–	–	–	–	–
Unemployed....................................	1,050	1,075	1,071	–	–	–	–	–	–
Unemployment rate.........................	7.8	7.8	7.7	–	–	–	–	–	–
Women, 20 years and over									
Civilian labor force.............................	9,965	9,907	10,018	–	–	–	–	–	–
Participation rate..............................	59.6	58.0	58.6	–	–	–	–	–	–
Employed..	8,938	9,107	9,192	–	–	–	–	–	–
Employment-population ratio..............	53.4	53.4	53.7	–	–	–	–	–	–
Unemployed....................................	1,027	800	826	–	–	–	–	–	–
Unemployment rate.........................	10.3	8.1	8.2	–	–	–	–	–	–
Both sexes, 16 to 19 years									
Civilian labor force.............................	1,051	1,130	1,075	–	–	–	–	–	–
Participation rate..............................	28.7	30.9	29.4	–	–	–	–	–	–
Employed..	734	821	817	–	–	–	–	–	–
Employment-population ratio..............	20.1	22.5	22.4	–	–	–	–	–	–
Unemployed....................................	317	309	257	–	–	–	–	–	–
Unemployment rate.........................	30.1	27.4	23.9	–	–	–	–	–	–

[1] The population figure are not adjusted for seasonal variation; therefore, identical numbers appear in the unadjusted and seasonally adjusted columns.

- Data not available.

NOTE: Persons whose ethnicity is identifie as Hispanic or Latino may be of any race. Updated population controls are introduced annually with the release of January data.

Table A-4. Employment status of the civilian population 25 years and over by educational attainment
[Numbers in thousands]

Educational attainment	Not seasonally adjusted			Seasonally adjusted					
	Nov. 2012	Oct. 2013	Nov. 2013	Nov. 2012	July 2013	Aug. 2013	Sept. 2013	Oct. 2013	Nov. 2013
Less than a high school diploma									
Civilian labor force.................................	11,072	10,604	10,937	11,097	10,889	10,939	10,860	10,730	10,932
Participation rate.................................	45.2	44.1	44.6	45.3	45.4	45.4	44.5	44.7	44.6
Employed...	9,762	9,525	9,784	9,753	9,692	9,700	9,743	9,564	9,756
Employment-population ratio................	39.8	39.6	39.9	39.8	40.4	40.2	39.9	39.8	39.8
Unemployed.....................................	1,310	1,079	1,153	1,344	1,197	1,239	1,117	1,166	1,176
Unemployment rate...........................	11.8	10.2	10.5	12.1	11.0	11.3	10.3	10.9	10.8
High school graduates, no college[1]									
Civilian labor force.................................	36,692	36,210	35,960	36,652	36,741	36,592	36,610	36,297	35,978
Participation rate.................................	59.5	58.3	58.3	59.4	59.0	59.0	59.0	58.4	58.3
Employed...	33,863	33,759	33,464	33,677	33,950	33,826	33,828	33,638	33,354
Employment-population ratio................	54.9	54.3	54.2	54.6	54.5	54.5	54.5	54.1	54.0
Unemployed.....................................	2,830	2,451	2,496	2,975	2,791	2,766	2,782	2,659	2,624
Unemployment rate...........................	7.7	6.8	6.9	8.1	7.6	7.6	7.6	7.3	7.3
Some college or associate degree									
Civilian labor force.................................	37,356	37,494	37,406	37,274	37,341	37,496	37,338	37,178	37,316
Participation rate.................................	68.6	67.4	67.8	68.4	67.3	67.2	67.2	66.8	67.7
Employed...	35,009	35,105	35,121	34,832	35,105	35,216	35,080	34,818	34,931
Employment-population ratio................	64.3	63.1	63.7	63.9	63.2	63.1	63.2	62.6	63.3
Unemployed.....................................	2,348	2,389	2,285	2,442	2,237	2,281	2,257	2,359	2,385
Unemployment rate...........................	6.3	6.4	6.1	6.6	6.0	6.1	6.0	6.3	6.4
Bachelor's degree and higher[2]									
Civilian labor force.................................	48,853	49,607	49,919	48,858	49,173	49,141	49,174	49,340	49,921
Participation rate.................................	75.5	75.4	75.2	75.5	75.5	75.4	75.3	75.0	75.2
Employed...	47,039	47,780	48,302	46,968	47,281	47,400	47,354	47,472	48,226
Employment-population ratio................	72.7	72.7	72.8	72.6	72.6	72.8	72.5	72.2	72.7
Unemployed.....................................	1,815	1,826	1,616	1,891	1,891	1,740	1,820	1,869	1,695
Unemployment rate...........................	3.7	3.7	3.2	3.9	3.8	3.5	3.7	3.8	3.4

[1] Includes persons with a high school diploma or equivalent.

[2] Includes persons with bachelor's, master's, professional, and doctoral degrees.

NOTE: Updated population controls are introduced annually with the release of January data.

HOUSEHOLD DATA

Table A-5. Employment status of the civilian population 18 years and over by veteran status, period of service, and sex, not seasonally adjusted

[Numbers in thousands]

Employment status, veteran status, and period of service	Total Nov. 2012	Total Nov. 2013	Men Nov. 2012	Men Nov. 2013	Women Nov. 2012	Women Nov. 2013
VETERANS, 18 years and over						
Civilian noninstitutional population	21,042	21,276	19,223	19,043	1,819	2,233
Civilian labor force	10,921	10,837	9,764	9,435	1,157	1,402
Participation rate	51.9	50.9	50.8	49.5	63.6	62.8
Employed	10,199	10,113	9,151	8,823	1,049	1,290
Employment-population ratio	48.5	47.5	47.6	46.3	57.6	57.8
Unemployed	721	724	613	613	108	112
Unemployment rate	6.6	6.7	6.3	6.5	9.3	8.0
Not in labor force	10,121	10,439	9,459	9,608	662	831
Gulf War-era II veterans						
Civilian noninstitutional population	2,575	2,963	2,144	2,319	431	644
Civilian labor force	2,121	2,429	1,813	1,965	307	463
Participation rate	82.4	82.0	84.6	84.7	71.3	72.0
Employed	1,909	2,187	1,642	1,770	268	417
Employment-population ratio	74.1	73.8	76.6	76.3	62.1	64.8
Unemployed	211	241	172	195	40	46
Unemployment rate	10.0	9.9	9.5	9.9	12.9	10.0
Not in labor force	454	535	331	354	124	181
Gulf War-era I veterans						
Civilian noninstitutional population	3,027	3,107	2,545	2,557	482	550
Civilian labor force	2,519	2,633	2,165	2,216	354	417
Participation rate	83.2	84.7	85.1	86.7	73.4	75.7
Employed	2,383	2,458	2,063	2,068	320	390
Employment-population ratio	78.7	79.1	81.1	80.9	66.4	70.9
Unemployed	135	175	102	148	34	27
Unemployment rate	5.4	6.6	4.7	6.7	9.5	6.4
Not in labor force	509	474	380	340	128	134
World War II, Korean War, and Vietnam-era veterans						
Civilian noninstitutional population	9,706	9,701	9,395	9,339	311	361
Civilian labor force	2,979	2,737	2,878	2,653	101	83
Participation rate	30.7	28.2	30.6	28.4	32.4	23.1
Employed	2,803	2,593	2,711	2,514	92	78
Employment-population ratio	28.9	26.7	28.9	26.9	29.4	21.7
Unemployed	176	144	167	139	9	5
Unemployment rate	5.9	5.3	5.8	5.2	9.1	6.1
Not in labor force	6,728	6,964	6,517	6,686	211	278
Veterans of other service periods						
Civilian noninstitutional population	5,733	5,505	5,139	4,827	594	678
Civilian labor force	3,303	3,039	2,908	2,600	395	438
Participation rate	57.6	55.2	56.6	53.9	66.5	64.7
Employed	3,104	2,875	2,735	2,470	369	405
Employment-population ratio	54.1	52.2	53.2	51.2	62.1	59.7
Unemployed	199	164	173	130	26	34
Unemployment rate	6.0	5.4	6.0	5.0	6.5	7.7
Not in labor force	2,431	2,467	2,231	2,227	199	239
NONVETERANS, 18 years and over						
Civilian noninstitutional population	214,099	216,254	93,938	95,425	120,161	120,829
Civilian labor force	142,232	142,265	71,672	72,055	70,560	70,210
Participation rate	66.4	65.8	76.3	75.5	58.7	58.1
Employed	132,060	133,143	66,399	67,210	65,662	65,933
Employment-population ratio	61.7	61.6	70.7	70.4	54.6	54.6
Unemployed	10,172	9,122	5,273	4,844	4,899	4,277
Unemployment rate	7.2	6.4	7.4	6.7	6.9	6.1
Not in labor force	71,867	73,989	22,266	23,370	49,601	50,619

NOTE: Veterans served on active duty in the U.S. Armed Forces and were not on active duty at the time of the survey. Nonveterans never served on active duty in the U.S. Armed Forces. Veterans could have served anywhere in the world during these periods of service: Gulf War era II (September 2001-present), Gulf War era I (August 1990-August 2001), Vietnam era (August 1964-April 1975), Korean War (July 1950-January 1955), World War II (December 1941-December 1946), and other service periods (all other time periods). Veterans who served in more than one war ime period are classifie only in the most recent one. Veterans who served during one of the selected war ime periods and another period are classifie only in the wartime period. Beginning with data for January 2013, estimates for veterans incorporate population controls derived from the updated Department of Veterans Affairs' population model.

Table A-6. Employment status of the civilian population by sex, age, and disability status, not seasonally adjusted

[Numbers in thousands]

Employment status, sex, and age	Persons with a disability		Persons with no disability	
	Nov. 2012	Nov. 2013	Nov. 2012	Nov. 2013
TOTAL, 16 years and over				
Civilian noninstitutional population................................	28,888	28,589	215,286	217,978
Civilian labor force..	5,990	5,590	148,963	149,456
Participation rate...	20.7	19.6	69.2	68.6
Employed...	5,230	4,900	138,320	139,875
Employment-population ratio................................	18.1	17.1	64.2	64.2
Unemployed..	761	690	10,644	9,581
Unemployment rate.......................................	12.7	12.3	7.1	6.4
Not in labor force...	22,898	22,999	66,323	68,522
Men, 16 to 64 years				
Civilian labor force..	2,751	2,485	75,035	75,372
Participation rate...	35.0	32.8	82.3	82.0
Employed...	2,353	2,110	69,526	70,300
Employment-population ratio................................	30.0	27.9	76.2	76.4
Unemployed..	398	374	5,509	5,072
Unemployment rate.......................................	14.5	15.1	7.3	6.7
Not in labor force...	5,100	5,084	16,174	16,585
Women, 16 to 64 years				
Civilian labor force..	2,187	2,255	67,037	66,745
Participation rate...	28.2	28.6	70.7	70.1
Employed...	1,920	1,985	62,263	62,595
Employment-population ratio................................	24.7	25.2	65.7	65.8
Unemployed..	268	270	4,774	4,150
Unemployment rate.......................................	12.2	12.0	7.1	6.2
Not in labor force...	5,571	5,624	27,763	28,419
Both sexes, 65 years and over				
Civilian labor force..	1,052	850	6,891	7,339
Participation rate...	7.9	6.5	23.5	23.8
Employed...	957	805	6,530	6,980
Employment-population ratio................................	7.2	6.1	22.3	22.6
Unemployed..	95	45	360	359
Unemployment rate.......................................	9.0	5.3	5.2	4.9
Not in labor force...	12,228	12,290	22,386	23,519

NOTE: A person with a disability has at least one of the following conditions: is deaf or has serious difficulty hearing; is blind or has serious difficulty seeing even when wearing glasses; has serious difficulty concentrating, remembering, or making decisions because of a physical, mental, or emotional condition; has serious difficulty walking or climbing stairs; has difficulty dressing or bathing; or has difficulty doing errands alone such as visiting a doctor's office or shopping because of a physical, mental, or emotional condition. Updated population controls are introduced annually with the release of January data.

HOUSEHOLD DATA

Table A-7. Employment status of the civilian population by nativity and sex, not seasonally adjusted
[Numbers in thousands]

Employment status and nativity	Total		Men		Women	
	Nov. 2012	Nov. 2013	Nov. 2012	Nov. 2013	Nov. 2012	Nov. 2013
Foreign born, 16 years and over						
Civilian noninstitutional population...............................	38,105	38,737	18,485	18,840	19,620	19,897
Civilian labor force...	25,217	25,579	14,384	14,802	10,832	10,777
Participation rate..	66.2	66.0	77.8	78.6	55.2	54.2
Employed...	23,272	23,961	13,410	13,920	9,862	10,040
Employment-population ratio...............................	61.1	61.9	72.5	73.9	50.3	50.5
Unemployed..	1,945	1,618	974	882	971	736
Unemployment rate...	7.7	6.3	6.8	6.0	9.0	6.8
Not in labor force..	12,888	13,158	4,101	4,038	8,788	9,121
Native born, 16 years and over						
Civilian noninstitutional population...............................	206,069	207,830	99,325	100,172	106,744	107,658
Civilian labor force...	129,737	129,467	67,925	67,595	61,811	61,872
Participation rate..	63.0	62.3	68.4	67.5	57.9	57.5
Employed...	120,277	120,814	62,732	62,806	57,545	58,009
Employment-population ratio...............................	58.4	58.1	63.2	62.7	53.9	53.9
Unemployed..	9,459	8,653	5,193	4,790	4,266	3,863
Unemployment rate...	7.3	6.7	7.6	7.1	6.9	6.2
Not in labor force..	76,333	78,363	31,400	32,577	44,933	45,786

NOTE: The foreign born are those residing in the United States who were not U.S. citizens at birth. That is, they were born outside the United States or one of its outlying areas such as Puerto Rico or Guam, to parents neither of whom was a U.S. citizen. The native born are persons who were born in the United States or one of its outlying areas such as Puerto Rico or Guam or who were born abroad of at least one parent who was a U.S. citizen. Updated population controls are introduced annually with the release of January data.

Table A-8. Employed persons by class of worker and part-time status
[In thousands]

Category	Not seasonally adjusted			Seasonally adjusted					
	Nov. 2012	Oct. 2013	Nov. 2013	Nov. 2012	July 2013	Aug. 2013	Sept. 2013	Oct. 2013	Nov. 2013
CLASS OF WORKER									
Agriculture and related industries................	2,045	2,263	2,050	2,121	2,159	2,204	2,209	2,209	2,132
Wage and salary workers[1]......................	1,274	1,415	1,258	1,320	1,303	1,367	1,397	1,356	1,309
Self-employed workers, unincorporated.......	761	800	754	776	842	820	772	795	778
Unpaid family workers...........................	11	48	38	–	–	–	–	–	–
Nonagricultural industries.........................	141,504	141,881	142,725	141,149	142,165	141,947	142,095	141,428	142,296
Wage and salary workers[1].....................	132,458	133,333	134,074	132,038	133,224	133,277	133,319	132,826	133,656
Government..................................	20,702	19,864	20,211	20,598	20,041	20,365	20,233	19,726	20,064
Private industries.............................	111,757	113,469	113,863	111,429	113,164	112,886	113,099	113,090	113,592
Private households..........................	754	796	849	–	–	–	–	–	–
Other industries.............................	111,002	112,673	113,014	110,659	112,535	112,244	112,434	112,313	112,744
Self-employed workers, unincorporated.......	8,977	8,492	8,589	8,959	8,831	8,678	8,634	8,531	8,551
Unpaid family workers..........................	69	57	62	–	–	–	–	–	–
PERSONS AT WORK PART TIME[2]									
All industries									
Part time for economic reasons[3]..................	7,994	7,700	7,563	8,138	8,245	7,911	7,926	8,050	7,719
Slack work or business conditions............	5,032	4,878	4,793	5,084	5,177	4,808	4,960	5,047	4,869
Could only fin part-time work..................	2,706	2,618	2,504	2,648	2,665	2,719	2,557	2,599	2,486
Part time for noneconomic reasons[4]..............	19,392	19,228	19,628	18,594	19,128	19,339	18,967	18,786	18,876
Nonagricultural industries									
Part time for economic reasons[3]..................	7,898	7,628	7,478	8,029	8,101	7,785	7,860	7,964	7,619
Slack work or business conditions............	4,975	4,832	4,738	5,025	5,106	4,747	4,896	4,998	4,811
Could only fin part-time work..................	2,685	2,611	2,494	2,650	2,665	2,714	2,556	2,601	2,473
Part time for noneconomic reasons[4]..............	19,043	18,866	19,320	18,310	18,779	18,935	18,696	18,432	18,633

[1] Includes self-employed workers whose businesses are incorporated.

[2] Refers to those who worked 1 to 34 hours during the survey reference week and excludes employed persons who were absent from their jobs for the entire week.

[3] Refers to those who worked 1 to 34 hours during the reference week for an economic reason such as slack work or unfavorable business conditions, inability to fin full-time work, or seasonal declines in demand.

[4] Refers to persons who usually work part time for noneconomic reasons such as childcare problems, family or personal obligations, school or training, retirement or Social Security limits on earnings, and other reasons. This excludes persons who usually work full time but worked only 1 to 34 hours during the reference week for reasons such as vacations, holidays, illness, and bad weather.

- Data not available.

NOTE: Detail for the seasonally adjusted data shown in this table will not necessarily add to totals because of the independent seasonal adjustment of the various series. Updated population controls are introduced annually with the release of January data.

HOUSEHOLD DATA
Table A-9. Selected employment indicators
[Numbers in thousands]

Characteristic	Not seasonally adjusted			Seasonally adjusted					
	Nov. 2012	Oct. 2013	Nov. 2013	Nov. 2012	July 2013	Aug. 2013	Sept. 2013	Oct. 2013	Nov. 2013
AGE AND SEX									
Total, 16 years and over............	143,549	144,144	144,775	143,277	144,285	144,170	144,303	143,568	144,386
16 to 19 years..........................	4,252	4,289	4,315	4,468	4,469	4,410	4,578	4,443	4,502
16 to 17 years........................	1,290	1,529	1,519	1,351	1,460	1,412	1,465	1,494	1,555
18 to 19 years........................	2,963	2,761	2,796	3,126	3,034	3,014	3,089	2,939	2,929
20 years and over....................	139,297	139,855	140,460	138,809	139,816	139,760	139,726	139,124	139,884
20 to 24 years........................	13,624	13,686	13,789	13,595	13,654	13,543	13,676	13,654	13,710
25 years and over....................	125,672	126,169	126,671	125,200	126,087	126,205	126,009	125,372	126,210
25 to 54 years......................	94,523	94,553	94,953	94,079	94,476	94,424	94,512	93,898	94,529
25 to 34 years....................	31,183	31,391	31,652	30,971	31,176	31,143	31,272	31,158	31,404
35 to 44 years....................	30,652	30,745	30,814	30,490	30,686	30,779	30,770	30,544	30,667
45 to 54 years....................	32,688	32,417	32,487	32,618	32,613	32,502	32,470	32,196	32,458
55 years and over..................	31,149	31,616	31,718	31,121	31,612	31,781	31,498	31,474	31,681
Men, 16 years and over................	76,142	76,403	76,726	75,983	76,466	76,164	76,452	76,074	76,541
16 to 19 years..........................	2,021	2,113	2,040	2,163	2,138	2,155	2,309	2,205	2,180
16 to 17 years........................	593	717	693	656	679	670	714	725	752
18 to 19 years........................	1,428	1,396	1,348	1,492	1,457	1,508	1,576	1,475	1,420
20 years and over....................	74,121	74,290	74,686	73,821	74,328	74,010	74,143	73,869	74,361
20 to 24 years........................	7,147	6,990	7,101	7,125	7,037	6,956	7,041	6,977	7,036
25 years and over....................	66,975	67,300	67,585	66,720	67,270	67,122	67,098	66,862	67,324
25 to 54 years......................	50,429	50,558	50,794	50,194	50,592	50,388	50,439	50,196	50,573
25 to 34 years....................	16,903	16,992	17,117	16,734	16,849	16,791	16,898	16,797	16,942
35 to 44 years....................	16,488	16,622	16,635	16,380	16,597	16,571	16,544	16,515	16,553
45 to 54 years....................	17,037	16,944	17,042	17,080	17,146	17,026	16,998	16,884	17,077
55 years and over..................	16,546	16,742	16,790	16,526	16,678	16,733	16,658	16,666	16,752
Women, 16 years and over..............	67,407	67,741	68,049	67,294	67,819	68,005	67,851	67,494	67,845
16 to 19 years..........................	2,232	2,176	2,275	2,305	2,330	2,255	2,268	2,239	2,322
16 to 17 years........................	697	812	826	695	781	741	751	769	804
18 to 19 years........................	1,535	1,364	1,448	1,634	1,577	1,506	1,513	1,464	1,509
20 years and over....................	65,175	65,565	65,775	64,988	65,489	65,750	65,582	65,255	65,523
20 to 24 years........................	6,478	6,696	6,688	6,470	6,617	6,588	6,635	6,678	6,674
25 years and over....................	58,698	58,869	59,086	58,480	58,817	59,084	58,912	58,510	58,885
25 to 54 years......................	44,094	43,995	44,159	43,885	43,884	44,036	44,072	43,702	43,956
25 to 34 years....................	14,280	14,399	14,535	14,237	14,327	14,353	14,374	14,362	14,461
35 to 44 years....................	14,164	14,123	14,179	14,109	14,089	14,208	14,226	14,029	14,114
45 to 54 years....................	15,651	15,473	15,445	15,538	15,467	15,476	15,472	15,311	15,380
55 years and over..................	14,603	14,874	14,927	14,595	14,934	15,048	14,840	14,808	14,929
MARITAL STATUS									
Married men, spouse present...........	44,293	44,162	44,480	44,016	43,914	43,988	43,744	43,778	44,131
Married women, spouse present.........	34,839	34,449	34,695	34,576	34,622	34,755	34,564	34,306	34,350
Women who maintain families...........	9,226	9,381	9,184	–	–	–	–	–	–
FULL- OR PART-TIME STATUS									
Full-time workers[1].....................	115,515	116,798	116,875	115,665	116,090	116,208	116,899	116,276	116,928
Part-time workers[2].....................	28,034	27,346	27,900	27,517	28,233	27,999	27,405	27,278	27,452
MULTIPLE JOBHOLDERS									
Total multiple jobholders..............	7,235	6,989	6,973	7,109	7,036	7,065	7,030	6,969	6,878
Percent of total employed.............	5.0	4.8	4.8	5.0	4.9	4.9	4.9	4.9	4.8
SELF-EMPLOYMENT									
Self-employed workers, incorporated...	5,160	5,423	5,330	–	–	–	–	–	–
Self-employed workers, unincorporated.	9,738	9,292	9,343	9,735	9,673	9,498	9,406	9,325	9,329

[1] Employed full- ime workers are persons who usually work 35 hours or more per week.
[2] Employed part-time workers are persons who usually work less han 35 hours per week.
- Data not available.
NOTE: Detail for the seasonally adjusted data shown in his table will not necessarily add to totals because of he independent seasonal adjustment of the various series. Updated population controls are introduced annually with the release of January data.

HOUSEHOLD DATA
Table A-10. Selected unemployment indicators, seasonally adjusted

Characteristic	Number of unemployed persons (in thousands)			Unemployment rates					
	Nov. 2012	Oct. 2013	Nov. 2013	Nov. 2012	July 2013	Aug. 2013	Sept. 2013	Oct. 2013	Nov. 2013
AGE AND SEX									
Total, 16 years and over.............	12,042	11,272	10,907	7.8	7.4	7.3	7.2	7.3	7.0
16 to 19 years....................	1,376	1,269	1,183	23.6	23.7	22.7	21.4	22.2	20.8
16 to 17 years.................	536	475	483	28.4	29.1	26.3	25.8	24.1	23.7
18 to 19 years.................	799	788	696	20.4	19.9	21.7	19.9	21.1	19.2
20 years and over..............	10,666	10,002	9,724	7.1	6.8	6.7	6.7	6.7	6.5
20 to 24 years.................	1,968	1,945	1,796	12.6	12.6	13.0	12.9	12.5	11.6
25 years and over.............	8,661	8,095	7,881	6.5	6.1	6.0	6.0	6.1	5.9
25 to 54 years..............	6,742	6,304	6,223	6.7	6.4	6.3	6.2	6.3	6.2
25 to 34 years...........	2,642	2,437	2,508	7.9	7.5	7.8	7.4	7.3	7.4
35 to 44 years...........	2,028	1,864	1,839	6.2	6.0	5.7	5.6	5.8	5.7
45 to 54 years...........	2,071	2,003	1,876	6.0	5.7	5.5	5.5	5.9	5.5
55 years and over..........	1,911	1,808	1,620	5.8	5.0	5.1	5.3	5.4	4.9
Men, 16 years and over.............	6,530	6,274	6,039	7.9	7.7	7.7	7.7	7.6	7.3
16 to 19 years....................	783	723	659	26.6	27.4	25.0	24.5	24.7	23.2
16 to 17 years.................	300	224	250	31.4	32.5	26.6	28.5	23.6	25.0
18 to 19 years.................	466	498	412	23.8	24.0	25.2	23.0	25.2	22.5
20 years and over..............	5,747	5,551	5,380	7.2	7.0	7.1	7.1	7.0	6.7
20 to 24 years.................	1,031	1,145	977	12.6	14.1	14.4	14.8	14.1	12.2
25 years and over.............	4,698	4,443	4,364	6.6	6.2	6.3	6.2	6.2	6.1
25 to 54 years..............	3,601	3,444	3,437	6.7	6.4	6.6	6.4	6.4	6.4
25 to 34 years...........	1,427	1,369	1,379	7.9	7.7	8.5	7.8	7.5	7.5
35 to 44 years...........	1,069	999	1,032	6.1	5.8	5.6	5.7	5.7	5.9
45 to 54 years...........	1,105	1,076	1,026	6.1	5.5	5.6	5.7	6.0	5.7
55 years and over..........	1,097	999	927	6.2	5.6	5.4	5.5	5.7	5.2
Women, 16 years and over.............	5,512	4,998	4,868	7.6	7.0	6.8	6.7	6.9	6.7
16 to 19 years....................	594	547	524	20.5	20.0	20.4	18.1	19.6	18.4
16 to 17 years.................	236	251	233	25.3	25.8	26.0	22.9	24.6	22.4
18 to 19 years.................	334	290	284	17.0	15.8	17.9	16.3	16.5	15.8
20 years and over..............	4,918	4,451	4,344	7.0	6.5	6.3	6.2	6.4	6.2
20 to 24 years.................	937	800	819	12.6	10.8	11.4	10.8	10.7	10.9
25 years and over.............	3,963	3,652	3,517	6.3	6.0	5.7	5.7	5.9	5.6
25 to 54 years..............	3,141	2,860	2,786	6.7	6.5	6.0	5.9	6.1	6.0
25 to 34 years...........	1,215	1,068	1,128	7.9	7.4	7.1	6.9	6.9	7.2
35 to 44 years...........	959	865	807	6.4	6.2	5.7	5.5	5.8	5.4
45 to 54 years...........	967	927	850	5.9	5.9	5.3	5.3	5.7	5.2
55 years and over[1]..........	773	800	661	5.0	4.9	5.2	5.1	5.1	4.2
MARITAL STATUS									
Married men, spouse present..............	2,184	2,078	1,951	4.7	4.3	4.3	4.4	4.5	4.2
Married women, spouse present..............	1,842	1,679	1,605	5.1	4.6	4.2	4.4	4.7	4.5
Women who maintain families[1]..............	1,103	982	982	10.7	10.5	11.0	8.8	9.5	9.7
FULL- OR PART-TIME STATUS									
Full-time workers[2]..............	10,155	9,693	9,243	8.1	7.6	7.6	7.6	7.7	7.3
Part-time workers[3]..............	1,810	1,579	1,632	6.2	6.2	5.6	5.8	5.5	5.6

[1] Not seasonally adjusted.

[2] Full-time workers are unemployed persons who have expressed a desire to work full time (35 hours or more per week) or are on layoff from full-time jobs.

[3] Part-time workers are unemployed persons who have expressed a desire to work part time (less than 35 hours per week) or are on layoff from part-time jobs.

NOTE: Detail for the seasonally adjusted data shown in this table will not necessarily add to totals because of the independent seasonal adjustment of the various series. Updated population controls are introduced annually with the release of January data.

Table A-11. Unemployed persons by reason for unemployment

[Numbers in thousands]

Reason	Not seasonally adjusted			Seasonally adjusted					
	Nov. 2012	Oct. 2013	Nov. 2013	Nov. 2012	July 2013	Aug. 2013	Sept. 2013	Oct. 2013	Nov. 2013
NUMBER OF UNEMPLOYED									
Job losers and persons who completed temporary jobs....................................	6,069	5,649	5,400	6,429	5,921	5,970	5,844	6,253	5,804
On temporary layoff.............................	877	1,059	912	1,080	1,221	1,062	1,087	1,535	1,158
Not on temporary layoff........................	5,193	4,590	4,488	5,349	4,700	4,908	4,758	4,717	4,647
Permanent job losers..........................	4,003	3,478	3,329	4,151	3,589	3,714	3,569	3,556	3,470
Persons who completed temporary jobs....	1,190	1,112	1,160	1,198	1,111	1,194	1,188	1,161	1,177
Job leavers..	913	883	874	926	979	893	989	861	893
Reentrants...	3,199	3,071	2,935	3,325	3,258	3,129	3,181	3,117	3,073
New entrants..	1,223	1,171	1,062	1,326	1,254	1,299	1,222	1,223	1,165
PERCENT DISTRIBUTION									
Job losers and persons who completed temporary jobs....................................	53.2	52.4	52.6	53.5	51.9	52.9	52.0	54.6	53.1
On temporary layoff.............................	7.7	9.8	8.9	9.0	10.7	9.4	9.7	13.4	10.6
Not on temporary layoff........................	45.5	42.6	43.7	44.6	41.2	43.5	42.3	41.2	42.5
Job leavers..	8.0	8.2	8.5	7.7	8.6	7.9	8.8	7.5	8.2
Reentrants...	28.1	28.5	28.6	27.7	28.5	27.7	28.3	27.2	28.1
New entrants..	10.7	10.9	10.3	11.0	11.0	11.5	10.9	10.7	10.6
UNEMPLOYED AS A PERCENT OF THE CIVILIAN LABOR FORCE									
Job losers and persons who completed temporary jobs....................................	3.9	3.6	3.5	4.1	3.8	3.8	3.8	4.0	3.7
Job leavers..	0.6	0.6	0.6	0.6	0.6	0.6	0.6	0.6	0.6
Reentrants...	2.1	2.0	1.9	2.1	2.1	2.0	2.0	2.0	2.0
New entrants..	0.8	0.8	0.7	0.9	0.8	0.8	0.8	0.8	0.7

NOTE: Updated population controls are introduced annually with the release of January data.

Table A-12. Unemployed persons by duration of unemployment

[Numbers in thousands]

Duration	Not seasonally adjusted			Seasonally adjusted					
	Nov. 2012	Oct. 2013	Nov. 2013	Nov. 2012	July 2013	Aug. 2013	Sept. 2013	Oct. 2013	Nov. 2013
NUMBER OF UNEMPLOYED									
Less than 5 weeks................................	2,340	2,585	2,155	2,596	2,563	2,563	2,596	2,761	2,461
5 to 14 weeks......................................	2,634	2,460	2,449	2,757	2,869	2,766	2,703	2,656	2,597
15 weeks and over................................	6,431	5,729	5,666	6,604	6,034	5,984	5,950	5,846	5,833
15 to 26 weeks.................................	1,724	1,772	1,677	1,820	1,788	1,694	1,804	1,782	1,766
27 weeks and over............................	4,707	3,957	3,989	4,784	4,246	4,290	4,146	4,063	4,066
Average (mean) duration, in weeks..............	40.1	36.5	37.9	39.7	36.6	37.0	36.9	36.1	37.2
Median duration, in weeks.......................	19.5	16.8	18.0	18.9	15.7	16.4	16.3	16.3	17.0
PERCENT DISTRIBUTION									
Less than 5 weeks................................	20.5	24.0	21.0	21.7	22.4	22.7	23.1	24.5	22.6
5 to 14 weeks......................................	23.1	22.8	23.8	23.1	25.0	24.4	24.0	23.6	23.8
15 weeks and over................................	56.4	53.2	55.2	55.2	52.6	52.9	52.9	51.9	53.6
15 to 26 weeks.................................	15.1	16.4	16.3	15.2	15.6	15.0	16.0	15.8	16.2
27 weeks and over............................	41.3	36.7	38.8	40.0	37.0	37.9	36.9	36.1	37.3

NOTE: Updated population controls are introduced annually with the release of January data.

Table A-13. Employed and unemployed persons by occupation, not seasonally adjusted
[Numbers in thousands]

Occupation	Employed		Unemployed		Unemployment rates	
	Nov. 2012	Nov. 2013	Nov. 2012	Nov. 2013	Nov. 2012	Nov. 2013
Total, 16 years and over[1].............................	143,549	144,775	11,404	10,271	7.4	6.6
Management, professional, and related occupations...........	54,951	55,583	2,077	1,749	3.6	3.1
Management, business, and financia operations occupations..................................	22,643	23,065	905	770	3.8	3.2
Professional and related occupations........................	32,308	32,518	1,171	980	3.5	2.9
Service occupations....................................	25,137	25,675	2,352	2,177	8.6	7.8
Sales and office occupations....................................	33,370	33,349	2,584	2,436	7.2	6.8
Sales and related occupations................................	15,632	15,683	1,236	1,173	7.3	7.0
Office and administrative support occupations..............	17,738	17,667	1,348	1,263	7.1	6.7
Natural resources, construction, and maintenance occupations....................................	12,986	13,092	1,516	1,224	10.5	8.6
Farming, fishing and forestry occupations..................	906	940	166	127	15.5	11.9
Construction and extraction occupations.....................	7,178	7,218	1,066	826	12.9	10.3
Installation, maintenance, and repair occupations...........	4,902	4,935	284	271	5.5	5.2
Production, transportation, and material moving occupations....................................	17,106	17,075	1,625	1,576	8.7	8.5
Production occupations.......................................	8,567	8,474	736	728	7.9	7.9
Transportation and material moving occupations...........	8,539	8,602	889	848	9.4	9.0

[1] Persons with no previous work experience and persons whose last job was in the U.S. Armed Forces are included in the unemployed total.
NOTE: Updated population controls are introduced annually with the release of January data.

Table A-14. Unemployed persons by industry and class of worker, not seasonally adjusted

Industry and class of worker	Number of unemployed persons (in thousands)		Unemployment rates	
	Nov. 2012	Nov. 2013	Nov. 2012	Nov. 2013
Total, 16 years and over[1]	11,404	10,271	7.4	6.6
Nonagricultural private wage and salary workers	8,600	7,882	7.1	6.5
Mining, quarrying, and oil and gas extraction	53	65	5.6	5.9
Construction	988	706	12.2	8.6
Manufacturing	982	984	6.4	6.2
Durable goods	640	617	6.6	6.2
Nondurable goods	341	368	6.1	6.4
Wholesale and retail trade	1,454	1,423	7.1	7.0
Transportation and utilities	398	410	6.6	6.7
Information	187	176	6.8	6.4
Financial activities	432	407	4.7	4.3
Professional and business services	1,197	1,164	7.9	7.5
Education and health services	1,176	890	5.2	3.9
Leisure and hospitality	1,354	1,212	10.3	9.0
Other services	381	443	5.7	6.8
Agriculture and related private wage and salary workers	193	131	13.6	9.7
Government workers	825	666	3.8	3.2
Self-employed workers, unincorporated, and unpaid family workers	563	530	5.4	5.3

[1] Persons with no previous work experience and persons whose last job was in the U.S. Armed Forces are included in the unemployed total.

NOTE: Updated population controls are introduced annually with the release of January data.

HOUSEHOLD DATA
Table A-15. Alternative measures of labor underutilization
[Percent]

Measure	Not seasonally adjusted			Seasonally adjusted					
	Nov. 2012	Oct. 2013	Nov. 2013	Nov. 2012	July 2013	Aug. 2013	Sept. 2013	Oct. 2013	Nov. 2013
U-1 Persons unemployed 15 weeks or longer, as a percent of the civilian labor force.........	4.2	3.7	3.7	4.3	3.9	3.8	3.8	3.8	3.8
U-2 Job losers and persons who completed temporary jobs, as a percent of the civilian labor force..........................	3.9	3.6	3.5	4.1	3.8	3.8	3.8	4.0	3.7
U-3 Total unemployed, as a percent of the civilian labor force (official unemployment rate)...	7.4	7.0	6.6	7.8	7.4	7.3	7.2	7.3	7.0
U-4 Total unemployed plus discouraged workers, as a percent of the civilian labor force plus discouraged workers.................	7.9	7.4	7.1	8.3	8.0	7.8	7.7	7.8	7.5
U-5 Total unemployed, plus discouraged workers, plus all other persons marginally attached to the labor force, as a percent of the civilian labor force plus all persons marginally attached to the labor force.........	8.8	8.3	7.9	9.2	8.8	8.7	8.6	8.6	8.3
U-6 Total unemployed, plus all persons marginally attached to the labor force, plus total employed part time for economic reasons, as a percent of the civilian labor force plus all persons marginally attached to the labor force......................................	13.9	13.2	12.7	14.4	14.0	13.7	13.6	13.8	13.2

NOTE: Persons marginally attached to the labor force are those who currently are neither working nor looking for work but indicate that they want and are available for a job and have looked for work sometime in the past 12 months. Discouraged workers, a subset of the marginally attached, have given a job-market related reason for not currently looking for work. Persons employed part time for economic reasons are those who want and are available for full-time work but have had to settle for a part-time schedule. Updated population controls are introduced annually with the release of January data.

Table A-16. Persons not in the labor force and multiple jobholders by sex, not seasonally adjusted

[Numbers in thousands]

Category	Total		Men		Women	
	Nov. 2012	Nov. 2013	Nov. 2012	Nov. 2013	Nov. 2012	Nov. 2013
NOT IN THE LABOR FORCE						
Total not in the labor force.............................	89,221	91,521	35,501	36,614	53,720	54,907
Persons who currently want a job............................	6,495	5,437	3,028	2,562	3,467	2,874
Marginally attached to the labor force[1]........................	2,505	2,096	1,267	1,080	1,238	1,016
Discouraged workers[2].....................................	979	762	556	471	422	290
Other persons marginally attached to the labor force[3]. ...	1,526	1,334	711	609	816	726
MULTIPLE JOBHOLDERS						
Total multiple jobholders[4]...........................	7,235	6,973	3,572	3,387	3,663	3,586
Percent of total employed.........................	5.0	4.8	4.7	4.4	5.4	5.3
Primary job full time, secondary job part time...................	3,752	3,575	2,014	1,960	1,738	1,615
Primary and secondary jobs both part time.....................	2,037	2,043	715	694	1,322	1,349
Primary and secondary jobs both full time.....................	218	212	128	128	90	84
Hours vary on primary or secondary job........................	1,172	1,117	678	592	494	524

[1] Data refer to persons who want a job, have searched for work during the prior 12 months, and were available to take a job during the reference week, but had not looked for work in the past 4 weeks.

[2] Includes those who did not actively look for work in the prior 4 weeks for reasons such as thinks no work available, could not fin work, lacks schooling or training, employer thinks too young or old, and other types of discrimination.

[3] Includes those who did not actively look for work in the prior 4 weeks for such reasons as school or family responsibilities, ill health, and transportation problems, as well as a number for whom reason for nonparticipation was not determined.

[4] Includes a small number of persons who work part time on their primary job and full time on their secondary job(s), not shown separately.

NOTE: Updated population controls are introduced annually with the release of January data.

Table B-1. Employees on nonfarm payrolls by industry sector and selected industry detail — Continued

[In thousands]

Industry	Not seasonally adjusted				Seasonally adjusted				
	Nov. 2012	Sept. 2013	Oct. 2013[p]	Nov. 2013[p]	Nov. 2012	Sept. 2013	Oct. 2013[p]	Nov. 2013[p]	Change from: Oct.2013 - Nov.2013[p]
Professional and business services - Continued									
Management of companies and enterprises. . .	2,023.6	2,048.6	2,054.5	2,057.5	2,020.6	2,049.2	2,054.9	2,056.8	1.9
Administrative and waste services............	8,276.0	8,639.8	8,695.5	8,658.9	8,119.3	8,474.5	8,495.7	8,510.4	14.7
Administrative and support services[1]........	7,901.6	8,257.5	8,315.5	8,280.8	7,744.7	8,095.3	8,117.5	8,131.6	14.1
Employment services[1]....................	3,324.4	3,519.4	3,565.7	3,574.4	3,201.6	3,430.6	3,442.9	3,457.1	14.2
Temporary help services...............	2,667.9	2,830.3	2,866.7	2,879.8	2,556.9	2,750.4	2,759.5	2,775.9	16.4
Business support services...............	850.8	851.6	869.0	879.7	834.1	856.1	858.9	862.0	3.1
Services to buildings and dwellings.......	1,850.4	1,956.9	1,940.7	1,898.5	1,841.6	1,891.2	1,892.5	1,891.4	-1.1
Waste management and remediation services..................................	374.4	382.3	380.0	378.1	374.6	379.2	378.2	378.8	0.6
Education and health services..................	20,675	20,664	20,964	21,048	20,460	20,756	20,786	20,826	40
Educational services..........................	3,529.2	3,314.2	3,532.5	3,580.7	3,351.6	3,378.6	3,386.5	3,397.4	10.9
Health care and social assistance............	17,145.4	17,350.2	17,431.3	17,467.3	17,108.0	17,377.8	17,399.1	17,428.7	29.6
Health care[3]................................	14,439.1	14,602.6	14,656.3	14,691.0	14,419.7	14,620.3	14,638.8	14,667.2	28.4
Ambulatory health care services[1]........	6,410.1	6,555.5	6,594.4	6,619.1	6,399.4	6,564.4	6,578.5	6,604.8	26.3
Offices of physicians..................	2,417.0	2,443.8	2,461.9	2,468.8	2,411.7	2,448.4	2,453.7	2,460.6	6.9
Outpatient care centers...............	666.0	698.8	703.1	706.0	667.0	701.6	702.8	706.6	3.8
Home health care services............	1,229.9	1,300.1	1,304.1	1,316.4	1,226.1	1,299.5	1,302.0	1,313.8	11.8
Hospitals.................................	4,824.0	4,829.8	4,836.2	4,843.1	4,820.7	4,834.6	4,835.7	4,836.9	1.2
Nursing and residential care facilities[1]....	3,205.0	3,217.3	3,225.7	3,228.8	3,199.6	3,221.3	3,224.6	3,225.5	0.9
Nursing care facilities..................	1,664.4	1,655.2	1,658.2	1,654.9	1,660.9	1,655.8	1,657.6	1,653.6	-4.0
Social assistance[1].........................	2,706.3	2,747.6	2,775.0	2,776.3	2,688.3	2,757.5	2,760.3	2,761.5	1.2
Child day care services.................	872.1	862.2	873.5	873.1	856.0	859.3	858.1	857.8	-0.3
Leisure and hospitality..........................	13,598	14,399	14,223	14,009	13,861	14,217	14,266	14,283	17
Arts, entertainment, and recreation...........	1,829.7	2,082.2	2,005.0	1,888.0	1,979.6	2,023.6	2,044.2	2,040.3	-3.9
Performing arts and spectator sports........	394.2	438.0	435.4	404.9	407.9	422.0	430.7	422.0	-8.7
Museums, historical sites, and similar institutions.	131.7	139.2	138.4	134.8	137.0	137.6	138.6	139.9	1.3
Amusements, gambling, and recreation.....	1,303.8	1,505.0	1,431.2	1,348.3	1,434.7	1,464.0	1,474.9	1,478.4	3.5
Accommodation and food services............	11,768.3	12,316.7	12,218.3	12,121.1	11,881.7	12,193.3	12,221.9	12,242.7	20.8
Accommodation............................	1,762.1	1,874.4	1,831.5	1,787.5	1,815.3	1,834.4	1,840.5	1,843.4	2.9
Food services and drinking places..........	10,006.2	10,442.3	10,386.8	10,333.6	10,066.4	10,358.9	10,381.4	10,399.3	17.9
Other services.....................................	5,452	5,482	5,492	5,489	5,464	5,491	5,495	5,499	4
Repair and maintenance......................	1,193.4	1,204.7	1,201.5	1,195.4	1,197.3	1,200.0	1,198.8	1,198.5	-0.3
Personal and laundry services................	1,326.2	1,344.6	1,347.5	1,346.8	1,327.0	1,344.2	1,349.6	1,346.7	-2.9
Membership associations and organizations...	2,932.7	2,932.5	2,943.0	2,946.4	2,939.4	2,946.9	2,946.2	2,953.3	7.1
Government...	22,352	21,741	22,208	22,320	21,879	21,864	21,850	21,857	7
Federal..	2,788.0	2,733.0	2,711.0	2,694.0	2,798 0	2,726.0	2,713.0	2,706.0	-7 0
Federal, except U.S. Postal Service.............	2,188.4	2,142.9	2,120.6	2,114.7	2,196.7	2,134.9	2,126.9	2,123.2	-3.7
U.S. Postal Service...........................	599.9	589.6	590.2	579.0	601.1	590.9	585.6	583.2	-2.4
State government................................	5,222.0	5,068.0	5,207.0	5,242.0	5,047 0	5,044.0	5,051.0	5,059.0	8 0
State government education.....................	2,576.4	2,417.3	2,558.8	2,593.1	2,390.5	2,389.2	2,392.1	2,398.1	6.0
State government, excluding educa ion..........	2,645.7	2,650.2	2,648.6	2,649.2	2,656.3	2,654.8	2,658.9	2,660.4	1.5
Local government................................	14,342.0	13,940.0	14,290.0	14,384.0	14,034.0	14,094.0	14,086.0	14,092.0	6.0
Local government education.....................	8,103.0	7,655.5	8,039.7	8,144.3	7,762.7	7,807.7	7,799.3	7,803.5	4.2
Local government, excluding education..........	6,239.3	6,284.3	6,250.6	6,239.7	6,271.1	6,286.6	6,287.0	6,288.1	1.1

[1] Includes other industries, not shown separately.
[2] Includes motor vehicles, motor vehicle bodies and trailers, and motor vehicle parts.
[3] Includes ambulatory health care services, hospitals, and nursing and residential care facilities.
p Preliminary

ESTABLISHMENT DATA

Table B-2. Average weekly hours and overtime of all employees on private nonfarm payrolls by industry sector, seasonally adjusted

Industry	Nov. 2012	Sept. 2013	Oct. 2013ᵖ	Nov. 2013ᵖ
AVERAGE WEEKLY HOURS				
Total private...	34.4	34.4	34.4	34.5
Goods-producing..	40.3	40.5	40.4	40.6
Mining and logging...	43.2	44.4	44.2	44.5
Construction..	39.0	39.1	38.8	39.1
Manufacturing...	40.7	40.9	40.9	41.0
Durable goods..	40.9	41.3	41.3	41.5
Nondurable goods...	40.2	40.2	40.2	40.2
Private service-providing...	33.3	33.3	33.2	33.3
Trade, transportation, and utilities........................	34.6	34.4	34.4	34.4
Wholesale trade..	38.5	38.6	38.8	38.9
Retail trade...	31.6	31.3	31.2	31.2
Transportation and warehousing........................	38.5	38.7	38.8	38.8
Utilities..	42.6	42.4	42.0	41.9
Information..	36.4	36.7	36.7	36.6
Financial activities...	37.2	37.2	37.1	37.2
Professional and business services.......................	35.9	36.1	36.1	36.2
Education and health services..............................	32.8	32.8	32.8	32.7
Leisure and hospitality.......................................	26.0	25.9	25.8	26.0
Other services..	31.5	31.6	31.6	31.6
AVERAGE OVERTIME HOURS				
Manufacturing..	3.3	3.4	3.4	3.5
Durable goods...	3.2	3.4	3.4	3.5
Nondurable goods..	3.4	3.3	3.3	3.4

p Preliminary

ESTABLISHMENT DATA

Table B-3. Average hourly and weekly earnings of all employees on private nonfarm payrolls by industry sector, seasonally adjusted

Industry	Average hourly earnings				Average weekly earnings			
	Nov. 2012	Sept. 2013	Oct. 2013[p]	Nov. 2013[p]	Nov. 2012	Sept. 2013	Oct. 2013[p]	Nov. 2013[p]
Total private..	$23.67	$24.09	$24.11	$24.15	$814.25	$828.70	$829.38	$833.18
Goods-producing....................................	24.84	25.32	25.34	25.40	1,001.05	1,025.46	1,023.74	1,031.24
Mining and logging.............................	28.93	30.01	30.27	30.43	1,249.78	1,332.44	1,337.93	1,354.14
Construction.......................................	25.93	26.20	26.23	26.24	1,011.27	1,024.42	1,017.72	1,025.98
Manufacturing....................................	24.03	24.53	24.54	24.61	978.02	1,003.28	1,003.69	1,009.01
Durable goods..................................	25.41	25.93	25.93	26.00	1,039.27	1,070.91	1,070.91	1,079.00
Nondurable goods.............................	21.66	22.10	22.11	22.19	870.73	888.42	888.82	892.04
Private service-providing..........................	23.39	23.79	23.82	23.85	778.89	792.21	790.82	794.21
Trade, transportation, and utilities...............	20.63	21.05	21.10	21.15	713.80	724.12	725.84	727.56
Wholesale trade................................	27.20	27.87	27.89	28.02	1,047.20	1,075.78	1,082.13	1,089.98
Retail trade.......................................	16.37	16.64	16.68	16.68	517.29	520.83	520.42	520.42
Transportation and warehousing..............	21.98	22.45	22.57	22.64	846.23	868.82	875.72	878.43
Utilities..	35.14	35.37	35.10	35.18	1,496.96	1,499.69	1,474.20	1,474.04
Information..	31.85	33.11	33.18	33.44	1,159.34	1,215.14	1,217.71	1,223.90
Financial activities...............................	29.66	30.38	30.38	30.44	1,103.35	1,130.14	1,127.10	1,132.37
Professional and business services.............	28.22	28.53	28.55	28.60	1,013.10	1,029.93	1,030.66	1,035.32
Education and health services....................	24.40	24.69	24.70	24.72	800.32	809.83	810.16	808.34
Leisure and hospitality...........................	13.39	13.54	13.54	13.51	348.14	350.69	349.33	351.26
Other services....................................	21.01	21.42	21.48	21.50	661.82	676.87	678.77	679.40

p Preliminary

Table B-4. Indexes of aggregate weekly hours and payrolls for all employees on private nonfarm payrolls by industry sector, seasonally adjusted
[2007=100]

Industry	Index of aggregate weekly hours[1]					Index of aggregate weekly payrolls[2]				
	Nov. 2012	Sept. 2013	Oct. 2013[P]	Nov. 2013[P]	Percent change from: Oct. 2013 - Nov. 2013[P]	Nov. 2012	Sept. 2013	Oct. 2013[P]	Nov. 2013[P]	Percent change from: Oct. 2013 - Nov. 2013[P]
Total private.....................................	97.0	98.7	98.8	99.3	0.5	109.5	113.3	113.6	114.4	0.7
Goods-producing............................	84.8	86.2	86.1	86.7	0.7	95.2	98.6	98.6	99.6	1.0
Mining and logging.......................	115.8	122.9	122.8	123.6	0.7	134.5	148.1	149.2	151.0	1.2
Construction................................	76.3	78.5	78.0	78.9	1.2	85.9	89.3	88.9	89.9	1.1
Manufacturing.............................	87.4	88.1	88.2	88.6	0.5	97.7	100.5	100.7	101.4	0.7
Durable goods..........................	86.2	87.6	87.7	88.3	0.7	97.2	100.9	101.0	102.0	1.0
Nondurable goods.....................	89.4	89.1	89.2	89.4	0.2	98.2	99.9	100.0	100.6	0.6
Private service-providing...................	100.6	102.4	102.3	102.8	0.5	114.0	118.0	118.1	118.7	0.5
Trade, transportation, and utilities.......	96.8	97.7	97.8	98.0	0.2	107.5	110.6	111.1	111.6	0.5
Wholesale trade........................	95.9	97.5	97.9	98.3	0.4	108.9	113.4	113.9	114.9	0.9
Retail trade..............................	96.3	97.0	97.0	97.1	0.1	104.2	106.7	106.9	107.1	0.2
Transportation and warehousing......	98.3	99.7	100.0	100.7	0.7	109.6	113.6	114.6	115.7	1.0
Utilities...................................	102.2	102.1	101.1	101.1	0.0	118.7	119.3	117.3	117.5	0.2
Information.................................	89.3	89.9	90.0	89.7	-0.3	101.2	105.9	106.3	106.8	0.5
Financial activities........................	95.3	96.3	96.1	96.3	0.2	110.2	114.1	113.9	114.3	0.4
Professional and business services.....	102.3	106.0	106.3	106.8	0.5	117.0	122.6	123.0	123.8	0.7
Education and health services...........	109.3	110.8	111.0	110.9	-0.1	124.9	128.2	128.4	128.4	0.0
Leisure and hospitality...................	102.8	105.1	105.0	106.0	1.0	111.1	114.8	114.7	115.5	0.7
Other services............................	95.4	96.1	96.2	96.3	0.1	113.7	116.9	117.3	117.5	0.2

[1] The indexes of aggregate weekly hours are calculated by dividing the current month's estimates of aggregate hours by the corresponding 2007 annual average aggregate hours. Aggregate hours estimates are the product of estimates of average weekly hours and employment.

[2] The indexes of aggregate weekly payrolls are calculated by dividing the current month's estimates of aggregate weekly payrolls by the corresponding 2007 annual average aggregate weekly payrolls. Aggregate payrolls estimates are the product of estimates of average hourly earnings, average weekly hours, and employment.

p Preliminary

ESTABLISHMENT DATA

Table B-5. Employment of women on nonfarm payrolls by industry sector, seasonally adjusted

Industry	Women employees (in thousands)				Percent of all employees			
	Nov. 2012	Sept. 2013	Oct. 2013ᴾ	Nov. 2013ᴾ	Nov. 2012	Sept. 2013	Oct. 2013ᴾ	Nov. 2013ᴾ
Total nonfarm.............................	66,398	67,393	67,468	67,562	49.4	49.4	49.4	49.4
Total private.................................	53,922	54,887	54,976	55,069	47.9	47.9	47.9	47.9
Goods-producing........................	4,100	4,105	4,114	4,127	22.2	22.0	22.0	22.0
Mining and logging....................	115	117	118	118	13.5	13.3	13.3	13.3
Construction............................	730	743	743	746	12.9	12.8	12.7	12.7
Manufacturing.........................	3,255	3,245	3,253	3,263	27.3	27.1	27.1	27.2
Durable goods......................	1,731	1,736	1,740	1,745	23.1	23.0	23.1	23.1
Nondurable goods.................	1,524	1,509	1,513	1,518	34.2	34.0	34.0	34.1
Private service-providing...........	49,822	50,782	50,862	50,942	52.9	53.0	53.0	53.0
Trade, transportation, and utilities..............	10,389	10,630	10,645	10,663	40.4	40.7	40.7	40.7
Wholesale trade..............................	1,708.0	1,727.0	1,718.8	1,716.8	29.9	29.8	29.7	29.7
Retail trade...................................	7,502.1	7,703.1	7,727.8	7,743.4	50.0	50.5	50.5	50.5
Transportation and warehousing.............	1,040.6	1,061.7	1,061.5	1,065.3	23.3	23.6	23.6	23.5
Utilities..	138.2	137.7	137.1	137.3	24.9	24.7	24.6	24.6
Information..................................	1,074	1,070	1,073	1,073	40.0	39.9	40.0	40.0
Financial activities...........................	4,536	4,543	4,543	4,539	58.0	57.5	57.4	57.4
Professional and business services...........	8,010	8,335	8,358	8,375	44.2	44.6	44.6	44.6
Education and health services.................	15,703	15,924	15,928	15,967	76.7	76.7	76.6	76.7
Leisure and hospitality.......................	7,234	7,392	7,424	7,431	52.2	52.0	52.0	52.0
Other services.................................	2,876	2,888	2,891	2,894	52.6	52.6	52.6	52.6
Government..	12,476	12,506	12,492	12,493	57.0	57.2	57.2	57.2

p Preliminary

ESTABLISHMENT DATA

Table B-6. Employment of production and nonsupervisory employees on private nonfarm payrolls by industry sector, seasonally adjusted[1]

[In thousands]

Industry	Nov. 2012	Sept. 2013	Oct. 2013[p]	Nov. 2013[p]
Total private..	93,041	94,522	94,729	94,886
Goods-producing...	13,306	13,416	13,452	13,481
Mining and logging...	638	649	653	652
Construction..	4,265	4,395	4,410	4,426
Manufacturing...	8,403	8,372	8,389	8,403
Durable goods..	5,161	5,166	5,177	5,182
Nondurable goods..	3,242	3,206	3,212	3,221
Private service-providing..	79,735	81,106	81,277	81,405
Trade, transportation, and utilities..................................	21,825	22,070	22,099	22,149
Wholesale trade...	4,603.7	4,668.7	4,665.6	4,668.1
Retail trade...	12,913.0	13,065.2	13,092.3	13,107.7
Transportation and warehousing....................................	3,863.3	3,886.7	3,890.7	3,922.3
Utilities...	444.7	449.8	450.6	451.2
Information..	2,172	2,176	2,177	2,173
Financial activities..	6,021	6,081	6,085	6,084
Professional and business services.................................	14,972	15,469	15,514	15,546
Education and health services..	17,941	18,188	18,218	18,258
Leisure and hospitality...	12,234	12,547	12,605	12,612
Other services...	4,570	4,575	4,579	4,583

[1] Data relate to production employees in mining and logging and manufacturing, construction employees in construction, and nonsupervisory employees in the service-providing industries. These groups account for approximately four-fifth of the total employment on private nonfarm payrolls.

p Preliminary

ESTABLISHMENT DATA

Table B-7. Average weekly hours and overtime of production and nonsupervisory employees on private nonfarm payrolls by industry sector, seasonally adjusted[1]

Industry	Nov. 2012	Sept. 2013	Oct. 2013[p]	Nov. 2013[p]
AVERAGE WEEKLY HOURS				
Total private..	33.7	33.7	33.6	33.7
Goods-producing...	41.1	41.4	41.3	41.5
Mining and logging...	45.4	46.2	45.4	45.8
Construction..	39.5	39.8	39.4	39.8
Manufacturing...	41.6	41.9	41.9	42.0
Durable goods..	41.9	42.3	42.4	42.5
Nondurable goods...	41.1	41.2	41.2	41.2
Private service-providing..	32.5	32.4	32.3	32.4
Trade, transportation, and utilities............................	33.8	33.5	33.5	33.5
Wholesale trade..	38.6	38.5	38.6	38.8
Retail trade..	30.5	30.0	30.0	29.9
Transportation and warehousing............................	38.2	38.5	38.5	38.5
Utilities...	42.2	42.2	41.3	41.4
Information...	35.8	35.9	35.7	35.6
Financial activities...	36.9	36.8	36.6	36.7
Professional and business services............................	35.2	35.3	35.3	35.4
Education and health services..................................	32.3	32.1	32.1	32.2
Leisure and hospitality...	24.9	25.0	25.0	25.1
Other services..	30.5	30.7	30.5	30.6
AVERAGE OVERTIME HOURS				
Manufacturing...	4.1	4.3	4.4	4.5
Durable goods..	4.1	4.4	4.5	4.5
Nondurable goods..	4.2	4.2	4.3	4.4

[1] Data relate to production employees in mining and logging and manufacturing, construction employees in construction, and nonsupervisory employees in the service-providing industries. These groups account for approximately four-fifth of the total employment on private nonfarm payrolls.

p Preliminary

ESTABLISHMENT DATA

Table B-8. Average hourly and weekly earnings of production and nonsupervisory employees on private nonfarm payrolls by industry sector, seasonally adjusted[1]

Industry	Average hourly earnings				Average weekly earnings			
	Nov. 2012	Sept. 2013	Oct. 2013[p]	Nov. 2013[p]	Nov. 2012	Sept. 2013	Oct. 2013[p]	Nov. 2013[p]
Total private...	$19.88	$20.25	$20.28	$20.31	$669.96	$682.43	$681.41	$684.45
Goods-producing......................................	21.05	21.29	21.32	21.36	865.16	881.41	880.52	886.44
Mining and logging.................................	26.13	27.03	27.15	27.33	1,186.30	1,248.79	1,232.61	1,251.71
Construction..	24.08	24.18	24.25	24.29	951.16	962.36	955.45	966.74
Manufacturing.......................................	19.17	19.36	19.38	19.40	797.47	811.18	812.02	814.80
Durable goods....................................	20.25	20.43	20.43	20.45	848.48	864.19	866.23	869.13
Nondurable goods...............................	17.40	17.59	17.63	17.66	715.14	724.71	726.36	727.59
Private service-providing............................	19.63	20.02	20.06	20.09	637.98	648.65	647.94	650.92
Trade, transportation, and utilities................	17.49	17.86	17.89	17.97	591.16	598.31	599.32	602.00
Wholesale trade.................................	22.40	22.76	22.82	22.93	864.64	876.26	880.85	889.68
Retail trade.......................................	13.84	14.10	14.11	14.17	422.12	423.00	423.30	423.68
Transportation and warehousing..............	19.44	19.96	20.05	20.10	742.61	768.46	771.93	773.85
Utilities...	32.18	32.41	32.44	32.43	1,358.00	1,367.70	1,339.77	1,342.60
Information..	27.24	27.95	28.01	28.13	975.19	1,003.41	999.96	1,001.43
Financial activities.................................	23.21	24.18	24.27	24.35	856.45	889.82	888.28	893.65
Professional and business services..............	23.40	23.70	23.74	23.74	823.68	836.61	838.02	840.40
Education and health services....................	21.19	21.56	21.58	21.61	684.44	692.08	692.72	695.84
Leisure and hospitality............................	11.65	11.83	11.85	11.80	290.09	295.75	296.25	296.18
Other services......................................	17.71	18.05	18.11	18.15	540.16	554.14	552.36	555.39

[1] Data relate to production employees in mining and logging and manufacturing, construction employees in construction, and nonsupervisory employees in the service-providing industries. These groups account for approximately four-fifth of the total employment on private nonfarm payrolls.

p Preliminary

ESTABLISHMENT DATA

Table B-9. Indexes of aggregate weekly hours and payrolls for production and nonsupervisory employees on private nonfarm payrolls by industry sector, seasonally adjusted[1]

[2002=100]

Industry	Index of aggregate weekly hours[2]					Index of aggregate weekly payrolls[3]				
	Nov. 2012	Sept. 2013	Oct. 2013[p]	Nov. 2013[p]	Percent change from: Oct. 2013 - Nov. 2013[p]	Nov. 2012	Sept. 2013	Oct. 2013[p]	Nov. 2013[p]	Percent change from: Oct. 2013 - Nov. 2013[p]
Total private....................................	104.7	106.3	106.2	106.7	0.5	138.9	143.8	143.9	144.8	0.6
Goods-producing............................	83.6	84.9	84.9	85.5	0.7	107.7	110.7	110.8	111.8	0.9
Mining and logging........................	153.9	159.3	157.5	158.7	0.8	233.9	250.5	248.8	252.2	1.4
Construction..............................	84.4	87.6	87.0	88.2	1.4	109.7	114.4	113.9	115.7	1.6
Manufacturing.............................	80.2	80.5	80.7	81.0	0.4	100.6	102.0	102.3	102.8	0.5
Durable goods..........................	81.3	82.1	82.5	82.8	0.4	102.7	104.7	105.2	105.7	0.5
Nondurable goods......................	78.5	77.8	78.0	78.2	0.3	96.5	96.7	97.1	97.6	0.5
Private service-providing...................	110.6	112.2	112.1	112.6	0.4	148.8	153.9	154.0	155.0	0.6
Trade, transportation, and utilities.......	102.8	103.1	103.2	103.4	0.2	128.3	131.3	131.7	132.6	0.7
Wholesale trade........................	104.7	105.9	106.1	106.7	0.6	138.1	141.9	142.6	144.1	1.1
Retail trade.............................	99.7	99.2	99.4	99.2	-0.2	118.3	119.9	120.2	120.5	0.2
Transportation and warehousing......	111.1	112.6	112.8	113.7	0.8	137.0	142.6	143.4	144.9	1.0
Utilities.................................	96.0	97.1	95.2	95.5	0.3	128.9	131.3	128.9	129.3	0.3
Information................................	88.7	89.2	88.7	88.3	-0.5	119.7	123.4	123.0	123.0	0.0
Financial activities........................	104.6	105.3	104.8	105.1	0.3	149.4	156.7	156.5	157.5	0.6
Professional and business services.....	118.1	122.4	122.7	123.3	0.5	164.5	172.6	173.4	174.2	0.5
Education and health services...........	125.0	125.9	126.2	126.8	0.5	174.1	178.5	179.0	180.2	0.7
Leisure and hospitality...................	111.6	114.9	115.4	116.0	0.5	147.6	154.4	155.3	155.4	0.1
Other services...........................	97.8	98.5	97.9	98.4	0.5	126.1	129.5	129.2	130.1	0.7

[1] Data relate to production employees in mining and logging and manufacturing, construction employees in construction, and nonsupervisory employees in the service-providing industries. These groups account for approximately four-fifth of the total employment on private nonfarm payrolls.

[2] The indexes of aggregate weekly hours are calculated by dividing the current month's estimates of aggregate hours by the corresponding 2002 annual average aggregate hours. Aggregate hours estimates are the product of estimates of average weekly hours and employment.

[3] The indexes of aggregate weekly payrolls are calculated by dividing the current month's estimates of aggregate weekly payrolls by the corresponding 2002 annual average aggregate weekly payrolls. Aggregate payrolls estimates are the product of estimates of average hourly earnings, average weekly hours, and employment.

p Preliminary

www.ingramcontent.com/pod-product-compliance
Lightning Source LLC
Chambersburg PA
CBHW080639290526
45790CB00007B/3126